Cambridge Elements

Elements in the Renaissance
edited by
John Henderson
Birkbeck, University of London, and Wolfson College, University of Cambridge
Jonathan K. Nelson
Syracuse University Florence

T0373859

RISKS IN RENAISSANCE ART

Production, Purchase, and Reception

Jonathan K. Nelson
Syracuse University Florence

Richard J. Zeckhauser
Harvard University

CAMBRIDGE
UNIVERSITY PRESS

Shaftesbury Road, Cambridge CB2 8EA, United Kingdom

One Liberty Plaza, 20th Floor, New York, NY 10006, USA

477 Williamstown Road, Port Melbourne, VIC 3207, Australia

314–321, 3rd Floor, Plot 3, Splendor Forum, Jasola District Centre,
New Delhi – 110025, India

103 Penang Road, #05–06/07, Visioncrest Commercial, Singapore 238467

Cambridge University Press is part of Cambridge University Press & Assessment,
a department of the University of Cambridge.

We share the University's mission to contribute to society through the pursuit of
education, learning and research at the highest international levels of excellence.

www.cambridge.org
Information on this title: www.cambridge.org/9781009476614

DOI: 10.1017/9781009402514

First published 2023

A catalogue record for this publication is available from the British Library

ISBN 978-1-009-47661-4 Hardback
ISBN 978-1-009-40253-8 Paperback
ISSN 2631-9101 (online)
ISSN 2631-9098 (print)

Risks in Renaissance Art

Production, Purchase, and Reception

Elements in the Renaissance

DOI: 10.1017/9781009402514
First published online: December 2023

Jonathan K. Nelson
Syracuse University Florence

Richard J. Zeckhauser
Harvard University

Author for correspondence: Jonathan K. Nelson, jnelso03@syr.edu

Abstract: This Element represents the first systematic study of the risks borne by those who produced, commissioned, and purchased art, across Renaissance Europe. It employs a new methodology, built around concepts from risk analysis and decision theory. The Element classifies scores of documented examples of losses into "production risks," which arise from the conception of a work of art until its final placement, and "reception risks," when a patron, a buyer, or viewer finds a work displeasing, inappropriate, or offensive. Significant risks must be tamed before players undertake transactions. The Element discusses risk-taming mechanisms operating society-wide: extensive communication flows, social capital, and trust, and the measures individual participants took to reduce the likelihood and consequences of losses. Those mechanisms were employed in both the patronage-based system and the modern open markets, which predominated, respectively, in Southern and Northern Europe.

Keywords: risk, patronage, rejection, social capital, trust

ISBNs: 9781009476614 (HB), 9781009402538 (PB), 9781009402514 (OC)
ISSNs: 2631-9101 (online), 2631-9098 (print)

Contents

1 Understanding Risks in the Renaissance

Preface

Risk was a recognized reality in the Renaissance. A raft of risks faced those who produced, commissioned, and purchased art in the Renaissance, but the profound impact of risk on the marketplace of goods, services, and ideas that enabled the Renaissance art business to thrive has not been investigated. Nevertheless, numerous studies published in the last few years by historians of premodern Europe have addressed the broader topic of risk (see Scheller, 2019a; Baker, 2021; Ceccarelli, 2021; each provides an extensive bibliography). As Nicholas Baker notes, the term *rischio* [risk] "peppered the correspondence of merchants across the Italian peninsula, a constant element in the calculation of the profitability and viability of any investment or speculation" (Baker, 2021: 97).

Baker's book focuses on a new conception about the future: around the year 1500, Italians started to see it as unknowable. An increased awareness of chance and change led to the belief that tomorrow might operate by different rules than today. Nevertheless, as Baker documents, the transformation in ideas about futurity hardly led to fatalist behavior. People still took actions to increase the possibility of success and diminish that of disaster. This realistic and pragmatic approach to the future underpins this study. This study's five sections discuss a widespread, but hitherto unstudied, phenomenon in the art world. Participants took actions to reduce the likelihood and consequences of risks in both the patronage-based system used across Europe and the more modern open markets that developed first in the North. Moreover, systemic developments, such as the evolution of artists' associations, helped to reduce risks to levels participants found acceptable. This volume employs a new methodology, built around concepts from risk analysis and decision theory. Specifically, it identifies the sources of losses suffered by artists, patrons, purchasers, and dealers. Those sources fall into two broad categories: *production risks* and *reception risks*. Production risks encompass the array of mishaps that occur from the time a work of art is conceived until its final placement. For artists working on a commission, the most frequent risk was delayed or insufficient payment. For patrons, late delivery of a painting or sculpture was the most common risk, but other documented hazards, still all too familiar today, included shoddy materials or practices, damages during transportation and installation, and forgeries.

Success in the art world required two steps: effective production followed by favorable reception. Reception risks arise when a patron, a buyer, or members of the intended audience found a work displeasing, inappropriate, or offensive. When we asked colleagues and students to name a consequential risk in the art world, most named public scorn. Such scorn generally emerged after a work of art was put on view in a palace, church, piazza, or marketplace. The criticism might be inappropriate imagery or substandard skill. Reception risks imposed financial and social costs that landed on artists, patrons, and buyers.

Sections 2 and 3 explore production and reception risks, respectively. Some risks are much harder to assess, or even foresee, than others. In response, our methodology distinguishes among reliable risk, uncertainty, and ignorance. Our primary focus is Italian art made between roughly 1400 and 1650, the period addressed in this series. Paintings and sculptures mentioned in contemporary records receive the greatest attention. Most of these works were commissioned to decorate ecclesiastical spaces, town halls and squares, and private palaces. These sections also address other geographic areas, including the open art market in Northern Europe. Germany and the Netherlands is the subject of Section 4, written by Larry Silver, a leading specialist of Flemish and Dutch art. The geographic emphasis of this study capitalizes, in part, on the plethora of published sources, and especially those by two celebrated sixteenth-century authors: Giorgio Vasari in Italy, and Karel van Mander in the Netherlands. Both wrote biographies of scores of artists; their accounts remain fundamental sources for Renaissance risks and failures. As noted by Patricia Rubin, "Vasari's portrayal of figures from the past was based largely on instructive probabilities, which abounded, not actual facts, which were limited ... Utility was the measure of Vasari's truth" (Rubin, 1995: 160). This "instructive probabilities" approach to history was followed by van Mander. Some of their stories are exaggerated, and others are probably invented. Nevertheless, all or most were considered plausible by their readers, including those of today. Their accounts, together with news about other risky art transactions, spread across Europe the knowledge about a wide range of losses.

The fifth and final section considers the fundamental role that trust played in pre-modern society, most notably in commercial interactions such as commissioning, buying, and selling art. Protagonists in the art world deployed an array of strategies to constrain risks. Three case studies illustrate three very different strategies in different centuries and regions. The analyses throughout this Element could have been made with examples of art made or sold in Spain, France, and England, to mention three major areas underrepresented in the discussions below. We expect that some readers could substitute the case studies discussed in this study with others from different time periods and areas of premodern Europe, and we hope that some will do so in the future.

Why, despite looming risks, did an increasingly large number of people acquire works of art? Because those works offered significant benefits for purchasers and patrons. Those benefits are explored in our earlier volume, *The Patron's Payoff*, which focuses on conspicuous art and architecture in Renaissance Italy (Nelson and Zeckhauser, 2008). These works allowed patrons and purchasers to honor their families, adorn their cities, and glorify God.

For Catholics, this last benefit was believed to shorten the patron's time in Purgatory. Equally important, and centuries before mass media and public relations agents made it easy, art helped patrons and owners bolster their reputations. We argued that the key players in the Renaissance art world weighed expected benefits against expected costs and concluded that the former outweighed the latter when they proceeded to commission art.

This Element focuses on the flip side of the coin: the risks of art and the costs these risks imposed. Even where open markets developed for prints and paintings – first in Northern European cities, and then in Italy and Spain – buyers confronted risks such as substandard materials or forgery. Everywhere a massive risk threatened, when governments fell or religious sentiments shifted, depictions of rulers or saints might be destroyed. Given the difficulty in mitigating production and reception risks, and of assessing those risks, many patrons, buyers, and artists expected to benefit from their activities, but wished in retrospect that they had chosen differently.

Selection Bias: Favoring Success

This volume counterbalances the widespread tendency to view the history of Renaissance art as a glorious sequence of successes. In that Pollyannish view, prominent individuals acquired works that delighted them and other viewers, and so the global patrimony expanded. But just as accounts of wars are disproportionately written by the victors, the successful fruits of Renaissance art production were far more likely to be prominently displayed, approvingly admired, and discussed in writing than those unsuccessful. From Amsterdam to Naples and Madrid, most pieces that survived their times and reached ours were regarded favorably by their original audiences. As a result, standard assessments of Renaissance art greatly underestimate the risks that were involved. The differential attrition of unsuccessful art produced what decision theorists call "selection bias." That concept applies whenever a sample of objects or beings, due to choices made by individuals or organizations, ends up being far from representative of the whole. Today, for example, worse drivers are more likely to purchase high-value collision insurance. As a result, a sample of such buyers has a greater fraction of poor drivers than the general population of motorists.

The biases favoring successful Renaissance art increased over multiple historical stages. First, pieces that displeased were often not put on view, hence less likely to be written about by contemporaries in treatises, journals, and guidebooks. Moreover, historical accounts tend to lose track of works that disappointed. The highly informed contemporary accounts by Vasari and van Mander show a different type of selection bias. When they wanted to present an artist as successful, they gave vastly more attention to works that avoided production problems and enjoyed a good reception. We strongly suspect that the writings of Vasari and Van Mander not only underrepresent failures for the period but also overrepresent them for artists and patrons they did not like.[1]

Second, documents relating to elite artists, patrons, collectors, and institutions – those who were more likely to succeed in the art game – had superior survival prospects. Indeed, archives hold far more documents about rulers than about their subjects. Moreover, the quantity and detail of records after 1500 far exceed those from earlier periods. Third, the records that do discuss art very rarely address social costs, such as the hazards of an unflattering portrayal. Fourth, modern scholars traditionally focus on the art and artists considered influential, interesting, and intriguing. The numerous exceptions to each of these observations hardly undermine the strong bias toward successful art in texts written from the Renaissance to our day. When compared to the most popular and written-about works of the period, an analytic tally of its disappointments, to follow, contributes to a more balanced assessment of failures and successes.

Histories of Renaissance Italy suffer from another selection bias: Florence gets undue attention. For the pre-modern period, more documents survive in Florence than in most other major European cities, though it was never a major political or military power. In part, Florentines seem to have been more assiduous record keepers than others. Moreover, attention is contagious. Since the late nineteenth century, art collectors and art historians have devoted more attention to works by Florentine artists than those from elsewhere. Given these forces, some observations about Italian Renaissance art and society undoubtedly reflect practices more prevalent in Florence than in other areas.

Premodern Understandings of Risk

Risk has been a central topic of discussion concerning finance, across many realms, for hundreds of years. In the United States, the Great Depression in the 1930s gave risk a starring role in discussions of macroeconomics and the economy. In the first years of the twenty-first century, however, many economists claimed that "the business cycle had been conquered." Risk regained prominence in the Great Recession of 2007–9. In recent years, and in studies around the globe, risk analyses have been widely applied to a vast range of topics. Climate change and pandemics have put the concept of risk front and center for both national leaders and ordinary citizens. Other events thrust risk references forward into sixteenth-century England. Shakespeare repeatedly used such phrases as "ten to one" or "twenty to one" (Bellhouse and Franklin, 1997).

---

[1] For the negative criticism of art in Vasari, see Franceschini (2021).

The bard's intended readers understood that these expressions indicated an intuitive, albeit imprecise, quantification of risk.

Risk was everywhere in Medieval and Renaissance Europe. Indeed, in some categories, such as illness and early death, it appeared in much greater abundance than today. Deep concerns for the uncertainties of the afterlife were the norm, given that one knew little about one's prospects for Heaven, or how much time one would have to spend in Purgatory. Then, as now, merchants and bankers had to face ordinary risks when acquiring assets, such as textiles or bank deposits, and then transforming and selling them as clothes or loans. Miscalculations could have dire consequences and, in many cities, both rich and poor suffered downdrafts and updrafts in their finances. A recent study argued, unexpectedly, that stability in relative wealth "was unusual rather than common among families in fourteenth- and fifteenth-century Florence" (Padgett, 2010: 371).

To better grasp a premodern understanding of risk, scholars have turned to a very large body of Medieval and Renaissance texts, analyzed extensively in recent decades by historians of economics, ideas, and society, but largely overlooked by students of cultural products. The concept of risk, and the term itself, first appears in documents from the mid-twelfth century and quickly spread across the Mediterranean region. In a commercial agreement from 1156, a certain Jordanus confirms that he received funds from Arnaldo Vacca which he would take to Valencia, and then possibly Alexandria in Egypt, in order to trade there "at your risk" (*ad tuum resicum*) (Scheller, 2019b: 3). James Franklin and Giovanni Ceccarelli have both clarified the fundamental importance of risk in juridical and theological discussions of usury dating from the late Middle Ages, two centuries before the works discussed in this volume (Ceccarelli, 2001; J. Franklin, 2001: 258–89). Shortly after 1200, Peter the Chanter argued that a buyer or a seller does not commit the sin of usury "if he exposes himself to the risk of receiving more or less" (J. Franklin, 2001: 263). Already in the late 1200s, in his influential volume, *On Sale, Purchase, Usury, and Restitution*, Peter John Olivi referred to the general agreement that "capital should profit him who runs the risk of it" (Ceccarelli, 2001: 614; J. Franklin, 2001: 263). Ultimately, this view reflects ancient Roman law, which established that those who bear risk should get the benefit. This understanding of risk, securely embraced by the modern theory of finance, is so familiar today that our only surprise may be to find it adopted in medieval Europe and earlier in ancient Rome.

Few people today read technical studies on risk and finance. However, through a process of intellectual osmosis from the worlds of economics and finance, the need for risk to be compensated now flows in the mainstream. Even in the Renaissance, that recognition flowed strongly in tributaries. Certainly, merchants learned some of these basic tenets in abacus schools, and churchgoers heard them expounded in sermons. San Bernardino, a highly popular Franciscan preacher in mid-fifteenth-century Italy, explained that risk-taking underpinned commerce, and provided the justification for legitimate profit (Ceccarelli, 2001: 621). Court decisions also upheld the principle that risk-taking deserved reward. This news circulated among merchants, bankers, and their clients.

In the past, as today, sophistication about risks varied significantly across the economy. Annuities and marine insurance, two financial instruments created in the 1300s, reflected the most developed understanding. Across Europe, but especially in Germany and the Low Countries, local governments often raised funds by accepting a sum of money in return for a stated annual income for life. In his 1307 *Treatise on Usury*, Alexander Lombard noted that the just price of an annuity could be established after considering "the age of the buyer and his health, and the risks concerning the profits from the possessions" (J. Franklin, 2001: 270–1). Even at this early date, financial players had identified risk factors, such as age and health, for pricing annuities.

For annuities and some forms of commercial insurance, most notably insurance on goods shipments, risk became commodified. This essential point was stated explicitly in numerous texts. In 1403, the Florentine jurist Lorenzo de Ridolfi wrote of insurance wherein "when you send your merchandise by sea or land to certain parts, and I take upon myself the risk and agree that for every 100 of value of that merchandise, you pay me a certain quantity of money . . . something is given for something done" (Ceccarelli, 2001: 620). This fundamental concept of risk as something concrete derives from the decision of Baldus, an earlier jurist, who wrote that no usury is involved where there is a genuine *quid pro quo*. One example is when "there is an accepting of risk, in return for giving something" (J. Franklin, 2001: 276). Surprisingly, though a highly advanced international market developed for marine insurance, policies were not generally available for ground transportation or for many other activities where risks lurked. Renaissance merchants and government officials thought about risk differently than we do today but, crucially for this study, individuals from many walks of life had risk on their minds.

Reliable Risk, Uncertainty, and Ignorance

The word "risk" embraces broad territory. To most people today, risk represents the broad category where outcomes are unknown and something of value may be lost.[2] We are all familiar with losses that involve money, such as sour investments or wrecked cars, that are readily compensable with money. However, some losses,

---

[2] In *Art and Risk in Ancient Yoruba*, Suzanne Blier focused on taking risks in the sense of experimentation. That led to her central thesis that risk spurred "artists (and patrons) into thinking about materials, techniques, and art forms in striking new ways" (Blier, 2015: 17).

such as the loss of one's good name, what Pierre Bourdieu (1984) famously called "symbolic capital," are difficult or inappropriate to measure in monetary terms.

For specialists in economics and decision theory, the term "risk" applies only in contexts where probabilities can be estimated with reasonable precision, such as for summertime weather. On television tonight, the weatherwoman might predict a 10 percent chance of rain tomorrow and, in reality, it will rain on just about 1 in 10 days. To express the same idea, a Renaissance sailor or farmer might say, less precisely, that rain was quite unlikely. In either case, the intended audience was aware of the risk and believed that it was established with some degree of reliability; thus, people could make plans accordingly. In the fifteenth century, for example, the city of Nuremberg created an early warning system for floods based on predictions made by observers upstream on the Pegnitz river (Scheller, 2019b: 6). Risk also applies to games with cards and dice. Significantly, these activities provided the bases for the first systematic study of probability, *The Book on Games of Chance*, written by the Italian mathematician Girolamo Cardano in the 1520s and revised in the 1560s but not published until 1663 (J. Franklin, 2001: 298).

The term "uncertainty," in contrast, indicates situations where the possible outcomes are known, but their probabilities are hardly known. This distinction was made by risk specialists only a century ago (Knight, 1921). Throughout the worlds of Renaissance art and finance or, for that matter, the world of today, situations characterized by uncertainty are common; situations of risk are rare. This volume uses "risk" in the colloquial sense: it applies the term to all situations where the outcome is unknown but the prime concerns are downside results. We introduce the term "reliable risk" for situations where either the probabilities are fully known, as with dice rolls, or where probabilities are closely estimable due to a great deal of experience, such as weather predictions. "Uncertainty" maintains its traditional use, to describe situations where probabilities are unknown, as say whether a particular commission will be fulfilled on time.

These categories generally align with the terminology of Giovanni Ceccarelli, the leading specialist on Renaissance marine insurance. He identifies two main categories of sea risks, "structural" and "contingent," based on his reviews of hundreds of extant policies and payments (Ceccarelli, 2021: 84–5). Structural risks are stable and predictable, such as the specific journey, the type of merchandise, and its degree of fragility. Contingent risks are based on factors subject to quick change, such as piracy. Most structural risks are reliable risks, and all contingent risks are uncertainties.

The usual way to gauge a reliable risk is to secure lots of data on similar situations. A successful cloth vendor, in the Renaissance or today, would know reasonably well the likelihood that a client can be nudged to a higher-priced fabric, or that such efforts will lose a sale. Similarly, the sale of standard products, such as prints, maps, or illustrated books, would offer enough experience to yield reliable risk assessments (Carlton, 2015). As discussed in Sections 2 and 4, at times a successful publisher or agent could accurately estimate the probability of finding a buyer for images depicting a particular genre or locale.

Regulations kept some grave dangers at bay. Across Europe, guild regulations prohibited painters from substituting expensive ultramarine with azurite or a mixture of the two (Kirby, 2000: 21). Artists had to know where to purchase materials of reliable quality. Repeat purchases and merchant reputations helped. In addition, several merchant handbooks even explained how to test ultramarine for its purity, thus helping to reduce the risk of deceptive substitution. These examples, where various instruments, actions, and techniques helped to trim uncertainties back toward reliable risks, represent exceptions. In the Renaissance world, few risks, whether of production or reception, offered the repeat experiences or the secure regulations that would enable them to be reliably assessed. Moreover, as noted by the sixteenth-century Florentine historian Vincenzo Borghini, "the nature of weights and measures is both very uncertain and very unstable. They vary from moment to moment, place to place and thing to thing, so much so that to reduce them to a fixed and equivalent term is very difficult, if not impossible" (Lugli, 2023: 3). Hard-to-predict human behavior or misbehavior was often the source of risk. All too often, situations were *sui generis*.

In his discussion of structural risk, Ceccarelli noted that insurance contracts and related letters provide very detailed information about merchandise to be shipped, and that insurers were aware of which objects were fragile or suffered from humidity. Unfortunately, the historical record cannot determine the impact of these reliable risks on premium rates. A parallel in the art world relates to Sebastiano del Piombo's *Pietà* (Madrid).[3] A letter from 1539 explains that the painting on slate was sent to its patron in Spain by sea because it was too fragile to transport by land with a mule train (Nygren, 2017: 63 n. 3). This illustrates a common trade-off where the risk for art is concerned. In this case, the greater risk of land travel outweighed its greater benefit of swifter delivery.

In the Renaissance art world, most production risks and all reception risks derived from uncertainties. Players could anticipate what hazards might arise but had insufficient means to assess their likelihood. Nevertheless, insurers took action to dim their risks. When marine insurers learned that pirates were active in a certain area, they demanded a higher premium from vessels traversing it. A Venetian document from 1457 neatly sums up the concept that the degree of risk determines the cost of premiums: "more risk equals more [higher] premium" (Scheller, 2019b: 4). Shippers could either pay up or select another route.

---

[3] Extant works of art in major collections are indicated only by the city.

Figure 1 Hans Memling, *The Last Judgment,* c. 1467–71, oil on panel, Muzeum Narodowe w Gdánsku, Gdánsk. Photo: Wikimedia.

Sometimes, the shipped merchandise included art, as in a well-documented case in 1473 concerning a galley traveling from London to Pisa. In addition to cloth and alum, it carried Hans Memling's *Last Judgment* (Figure 1), an altarpiece commissioned by Angelo Tani in Bruges for his chapel in Florence. After pirates attacked the ship, they brought all the booty to their native Gdansk. The altarpiece, never liberated, stands there today (Daniels and Esch, 2021: 671–2).

Van Mander (1994: 85) recounted a shipping mishap, where action reduced the risk. When Rogier van der Weyden's *Deposition* (Madrid; Figure 2) was sent from Flanders to the King of Spain, the ship sank. Fortunately, the painting "was fished out and because it was very tightly and well packed it was not damaged too much." Van Mander's readers not only knew about the uncertainties of marine transportation but also how losses could be reduced by selecting safer routes and by packing goods more securely.

Reliable risks and uncertainty apply when potential hazards are known. Many hazards arise from causes that cannot be identified in advance, or perhaps could be identified but are not. Economists have recently coined the term "ignorance" for these situations, which occur very often in the art world when some possible outcomes are unknown or unknowable (Zeckhauser, 2006; Roy and Zeckhauser, 2015). For example, in 2019, virtually no one envisioned a pandemic that would shut down the world; a half millennium earlier, virtually no one could foresee the Reformation-inspired iconoclasm in German churches.

Figure 2 Roger van der Weyden, *Deposition*, before 1443, oil on panel, Museo
Nacional del Prado, Madrid. Photo: Wikimedia.

The sociologist Niklas Luhmann (2002) distinguished risk from danger,
focusing on predictability. The first dealt with predictable unknowns, the latter
with "unknown unknowns," akin to what Knight first labelled uncertainty.
Luhmann was not concerned with situations where even the state of the world
could not be foreseen, what we label ignorance. He focused on risks that flowed
from the decision made by a group or individual, as opposed to, say, natural
(floods) or societal (inflations) causes. To understand risk in an historical
context, as Suzanne Reichlin rightly noted, social motivation, interpretation,
and assessment must complement Luhmann's concepts (Reichlin, 2019).

To summarize, we identify three classes of risk: reliable risk (probabilities
can be reasonably assessed); uncertainty (probabilities hard or impossible to
assess); and ignorance (even possible outcomes are not known). Given that few
situations in the Renaissance art world can be considered reliable risks, the latter
two classes animate this volume. Players were very aware of many uncertainties
and could try to avoid negative outcomes. However, when ignorance reigned,
planning slept.

A recurring but often unimagined development was the destruction of monu-
ments following a revolution in religion or rule. The most significant Renaissance

Figure 3 Agostino di Giovanni and Agnolo di Ventura, *Monument to Guido Tarlati* (detail), 1330, marble, Cathedral, Arezzo. Photo: Wikimedia.

example was the Protestant Reformation. Its significant role in the removal and destruction of art is explored in Section 4. Political upheavals could lead to an official *damnatio memoriae*, or the condemnation of memory. In 1340, popular sentiment in Arezzo turned against its long-deceased former lord and bishop, Guido Tarlati (Figure 3). His opponents attacked his marble tomb in the cathedral and chipped off his image in the scenes celebrating events from his life. (The portraits were restored in the eighteenth century; Pelham, 2000.) Similarly, in 1506, Giovanni Bentivoglio, Lord of Bologna, was expelled. This inspired the demolition of his family palace and the subsequent loss of several paintings by both Lorenzo Costa and Francesco Francia (Vasari, 1912–15, 3:163, 4:25). Bentivolgio's fall also led to the destruction of two statues of Pope Julius II: Michelangelo's bronze at San Petronio and Alfonso Lombardi's stucco work at the town hall (Hendler, 2021: 121). Papal portraits were not safe, even in Rome. Soon after the death of Pope Paul IV, in 1559, civic officials had a stonecutter cut off the nose, ears, and right arm of a marble statue of him. After the head was severed, it was cursed and mocked by children (Hunt, 2016: 186–7).

Ignorance is often associated with much less dramatic events. The remodeling of a palace or church often led to works destroyed, as happened to the Vatican frescoes made for Pope Nicholas V by Piero della Francesca and Fra Angelico. They were demolished by renovations dictated by Pope Julius II and

Paul III, respectively (Vasari, 1912–15, 3:18, 32). Neither the original patrons nor the artists foresaw the potential for such losses; hence they made no plans to avoid them.

We review our two categories of risk sources – production and reception – and our three classes describing its properties – reliable risk, uncertainty, and ignorance – with the salient example of the altar wall of the Sistine Chapel. For reasons both religious and artistic, this is among the most important and celebrated chapels in Christendom. Popes commissioned the decorations, usually by highly esteemed artists. Significant negative outcomes were less likely to be experienced here because the stakes were high, the patrons powerful, and the artists highly skilled. Yet here too risks abounded.

The original fresco altarpiece of the Sistine Chapel seemingly presented little risk. Commissioned in about 1481 by Pope Sixtus IV from Pietro Perugino, the subject closely corresponded to the fresco that Perugino had recently completed in the nearby church of St. Peter's. The artist had an established track record even before he came to Rome, so the patron knew what he was getting. Yet, this same work also illustrates ignorance: Neither Sixtus IV nor Perugino could have imagined that only a few decades after the altarpiece was unveiled, Pope Paul III would have Michelangelo destroy it to make room for his new painting, the *Last Judgment* (Figure 4).

The *Last Judgment*, in turn, encountered significant production and reception risks. According to Vasari (1912–15, 6:185), Michelangelo's friend Fra Sebastiano del Piombo persuaded the Pope that Michelangelo should paint the *Last Judgment* in oil on plaster, a new technique that Sebastiano himself developed. Michelangelo remained noncommittal, which should have alerted all to the risk of a negative outcome. Finally, Sebastiano prepared the wall for oil painting, then Michelangelo waited "some months without setting his hand to the work. But at last, after being pressed, he said that he would only do it in fresco," and the "incrustation" applied by Sebastiano was removed. According to documents, this took place in 1536, and the *Last Judgment* was completed in 1541 (Mancinelli, 1997: 160).

The stylistic and iconographic innovations in the fresco dramatically raised the possibility of reception risks. Shortly after the Sistine Chapel altar wall was unveiled, the secretary of Cardinal Ercole Gonzaga, Nino Sernini, wrote that there was "no lack of those who condemn it." He noted one criticism shared by numerous contemporaries: Michelangelo "made Christ beardless and too young, and that he does not possess the appropriate majesty." Fifty years later, in 1591, Gregorio Comanini wrote that the lack of a beard was considered by some to be an error because "theologians teach us that men have to be resurrected with beards and as mature as our Savior when he died" (Barnes, 1998: 78, 100). These

Figure 4 Michelangelo, *The Last Judgment,* 1534–41, fresco, Sistine Chapel, Vatican City. Photo: Wikimedia.

viewers and many others (Freedman, 2015: 24–5), it seems, neither understood nor appreciated Michelangelo's innovative representation, which gave Christ the dignity of an ancient god. Significantly, Christ's beard appears in several otherwise faithful copies of Michelangelo's fresco dating from the sixteenth century (Agosti, 1989: 1293). A few decades later, Pirro Ligorio attacked an unnamed painter, evidently Michelangelo in his *Last Judgment,* who represented overly muscular women, and who showed male and female figures, adults and children, and angels and devils in too similar a fashion (Schreurs, 2000: 410; on "artistic innovation as a problem," also see van Kessel, 2017: 96–103). This criticism explicitly attacked the artist's skill. Indeed, the nudity of many saints in the *Last Judgment* spurred the best-known criticism of Michelangelo's fresco. Dramatic consequences followed: Starting in 1564, two figures were repainted, and clothing was added to about forty more. The loss to Michelangelo's original conception was minor relative to the greatest danger it faced. As we will see in Section 3, many of the criticisms related to reforms associated with the Council of Trent, and several Renaissance observers even recommended that the fresco be destroyed.

Renaissance Risk Assessment

In Renaissance Europe, the winds of fortune tossed people from all walks of life. Merchants and bankers, for example, frequently mentioned hazards in their writings, and struggled to limit those risks. Many understood the familiar principle already articulated in the fourteenth-century French proverb: "He who never undertook anything never achieved anything." Every merchant who launched an undertaking or purchased goods to be resold later had to weigh benefits and costs, however informally. Are the odds that I can resell the goods for a significant markup great enough to justify the risk of buying and holding them? And, if so, how should the price reflect the risk that they may get stolen or damaged? The presence of risk was well understood; how to deal with it was much less so. Similarly, in the art world, risks abounded, and a venturesome approach was required to have prospects of success in any role.

In comparison to merchants and bankers today, those working in the Early Modern period faced at least three significant obstacles to confronting risk effectively. First, insurance calculations were primitive, as data sets were minuscule relative to those today for, say, life expectancy or shipping risks. Moreover, there is no evidence that Renaissance insurance rates were set based on anything close to statistical analyses. Even in today's insurance world, lack of data leads to grave consequences, such as when Lloyds of London collapsed in the 1990s due to completely unforeseen levels of asbestos liability. Second, much of the information necessary to make decisions was based on inaccurate instruments, such as faulty compasses or discredited beliefs. If you do not understand weather systems or illnesses, it is difficult to create appropriate insurance policies. If you agree with the fifteenth-century architect Filarete that the stability of buildings is based not only on "the goodness of the material," but also "the sign or planet under which it was built" (Hub, 2011: 23), you hire an astrologer to select the most auspicious time and date to begin construction. This method for reducing production risks was once common for major Renaissance buildings. Alas, believing in celestial charts for new buildings does not make them any more effective. Third, our modern tools for displaying information had not yet been invented. Only in 1620 did Michael Florent van Langren, a Dutch cartographer, create the first chart of statistical data, an innovation that allowed one to easily trace information points across time (Friendly and Wainer, 2021). Without the line graph, bar chart, and pie chart to facilitate comparison, it is difficult to distill informative patterns from individual case histories.

Several additional factors made risks particularly hard to gauge in the Renaissance art world. First, paintings and sculptures varied greatly, far more than many other products in an age that long preceded mass standardization. One found greater variation among portraits than, say, among clocks or beds. Such variability reduced the value of experience in judging risks. Second, most people active in the art world made few purchases. Though the most esteemed buyers might acquire many works of art, these would typically include only one or two of a particular type, such as altarpieces, fresco cycles, or sculpted busts. Third, while artists often provided preliminary drawings of commissioned works, visits to artists' studios were rare; hence, most patrons acquired finished products sight unseen. If patrons were displeased, their artists faced an increased risk of reduced payment, requests for changes, or even rejection. The confluence of these factors imposed further risks on participants in the art world: they were severely limited in their ability to assess the risks they faced. Even with today's sophisticated risk-assessment tools, none of these factors can be analyzed statistically. Rather, individuals would have to assess them using subjective or personal probabilities. That concept was not even recognized until the twentieth century (Ramsey, 1931).

The related field of behavioral decision theory first received significant attention in the 1970s.[4] Its principal finding is that individuals regularly make poor decisions, particularly when facing uncertainties. Now widely accepted, this conclusion contrasted sharply with the then-standard assumption in economics that people choose reasonably rationally. Similar shortcomings in decision-making were at play in the Renaissance period. Moreover, what we think of today as "modern science," with its careful attention to painstaking observation and causal reasoning, had not been developed. At the beginning of the seventeenth century, Galileo pioneered such methods, but his era hardly embraced him. Even research based on careful observation with telescopes was risky business in the Renaissance.

Certainly, all the participants in the Renaissance art world had to grapple with informal risk weightings. Some people were better at this than others. Most of the major patrons and collectors had succeeded in other realms where reasonably effective weighing of risks was critical to success. Those who failed or fell

---

[4] The field was pioneered by psychologists Daniel Kahneman and Amos Tversky (Kahneman and Tversky, 1974; Kahneman and Tversky, 1979). Tversky died in 1996; Kahneman was awarded the Nobel Prize in Economics in 2002.

short in business rarely had the resources to commission or purchase art. Leaders in governments and churches, the most frequent patrons of major commissions in architecture, painting, and sculpture, often addressed risks in their regular activities, which gave them some training and insight. Moreover – and this important detail is often overlooked – elite patrons regularly engaged intermediaries with business experience and broad exposure to the business of art to advise them on or to handle their deals. The most fundamental requirement for limiting risk is to assess potential dangers with reasonable accuracy. For patrons, it is far more valuable to identify the artist who regularly delivers on time than to write a contract with a payment claw-back should a producer prove unreliable. That said, it was still valuable to introduce risk-limiting measures in these dealings, such as contracts, evaluating committees that ruled on whether payments should be reduced, and the use of preliminary drawings.

Some players capitalized effectively on their superior ability to calculate risks. Lucas Luce, for example, a dealer active in late sixteenth-century Amsterdam, purchased untitled and unattributed paintings at auction for low prices and then, working as an arbitrageur, resold them to new buyers (Montias, 2002: 120). Luce prospered by taking on well-calculated risks. However, those dealers who calculated poorly, and there were many, met failure.

Artists too had to engage in informal risk weightings, say in deciding how much to charge. Ask for too much, and a commission or sale might be lost. If you work for a patron, you have timing risks: underestimate the time required for a project, and you run the risk of late delivery which will anger your patron. The production process itself included countless assessments of risk and the decisions that followed. Attempt innovation in style or technique? Pay the price for the highest quality materials – and whom to trust when buying materials? How much work to delegate to assistants, given the threat that poses to quality? Make the wrong decisions and time, money, and status could be lost.

Mistakes in taking risks are of two main types: taking risks that one shouldn't, and not taking risks that one should. Of the two, it is far more difficult to document risks mistakenly foregone. But we do have an example where too much and too little reception risk was taken by the same artist. Fra Bartolomeo, a Florentine painter usually associated with conventional representations of religious subjects, traveled in 1508 to Venice and signed a contract with Bartolomeo d'Alzano, prior of San Pietro Martire, for an altarpiece depicting the marriage of Saint Catherine of Siena. The artist and patron probably agreed on the highly unusual iconography of the painting, completed just a year later. By this time, however, the prior had already died, and his successor evidently did not like the work. He refused to pay Fra Bartolomeo, then commissioned a less expensive and very conventional painting by a minor local painter, Francesco Bissolo. In the end, Fra Bartolomeo donated the rejected altarpiece to a friend and prior in Lucca, who installed the work in the church of San Romano (Ekserdjian, 2021: 40; Nova, 2021: 9–10). Perhaps this stinging experience prompted Fra Bartolomeo to play it too safe that same year when he produced what must have been a rather conventional *Madonna* for Averardo Salviati. A 1509 letter from the patron indicates that he objected on aesthetic grounds. He was displeased because the work is very ordinary and "new things are always more beautiful"; the work was returned (D. Franklin, 2001: 94).

In the Renaissance art world, uncertain outcomes could prove a blessing or a blow. This volume focuses on the latter. It recounts a litany of the losses that participants in the art world suffered, from paintings purloined to statues scorned.

2 Production Risks: Sources and Their Control

Many cultural products elicit fascination in process; witness the popularity of "backstage" videos about the creation of films or albums. In textbooks and popular publications, interest in Renaissance art focuses on the finished product. Over the last half-century, however, many Renaissance art historians have turned their attention to the complex networks of individuals and processes involved in the creation of paintings and sculptures. A recent study elucidates how broad that network was. In the later sixteenth century, the cost of sending the king of Spain a marble statue from Florence included payment

> for the procurement of marble, for the sculptor to make it, for it to be properly packaged, for it to be delivered to a seaport, for it to be loaded onto a galley or other vessel, for the shipment by sea, for the oxen, carts, and men to transport it to Madrid, for passports and customs fees, and for the labor, meals, and sometimes clothing for the workers who accompanied the sculpture, delivered it to the court, and set it into place (Helmstutler di Dio, 2015: 177).

Production networks produce extraordinary results when information and materials pass reliably from node to node, as happens in most parts of contemporary economies. The production of art in the Renaissance faced a range of reliability problems, from miscommunication and misrepresentation to subcontracting and sunken ships. This section surveys the various mishaps that could and did occur from the artist's conception of a work to its final placement. Scores of documented examples show that people in the Renaissance knew about production risks for art and made decisions aimed to mitigate them.

Trust was a major mitigating measure. The concept of trust, often discussed by economists and sociologists, but much less by art historians, is a key instrument for bringing otherwise insurmountable production risks down to an acceptable level. In his *Foundations of Social Theory*, James Coleman argued that the incorporation of risk into decision-making "can be described by the single word 'trust.' Situations involving trust constitute a subclass of those involving risk. They are situations in which the risk one takes depends on the performance of another actor" (Coleman, 1990: 101). In other risky situations, nature is the prime actor.

The success of the Renaissance art market derived in no small part from the spread of trust among its participants: artists and patrons, buyers, dealers, and suppliers. Spreading trust in this setting reflected, capitalized on, and supported faith in a broad array of Renaissance institutions. But why did trust exist given the widespread losses discussed in these pages, many due to the misbehavior of individuals, and the multitude of losses not even mentioned? The reason is that it is often a reasonable strategy to trust an individual who may turn out not to merit trust, that is, who turns out not to be trustworthy. Any dealings with an individual, today as in the Renaissance, involves some element of a gamble. Reputations and legal remedies – both intended to deter bad behavior – are helpful in shifting the odds in a strongly favorable direction. However, even if losses remained a real possibility, a transaction should go forward if the potential gains outweigh the risk of losses.

Renaissance societies experienced high levels of transactions for many things, such as sales of cloth and insurance policies, with individuals and firms on both sides of the market. These transactions, which yielded information about the reliability of participants, made it important for participants to protect their reputations. "Strong ties" typically existed among close relatives or between merchants and repeat buyers, such as artists and repeat patrons. If participants in a transaction knew one another, perhaps from a few low-value business transactions or from a distant family relationship, they had what specialists call a "weak tie." A single tie was not nearly sufficient to generate trust. In his study of "What a Merchant's Errant Son Can Teach Us about the Dynamics of Trust," Ricardo Court examined a series of letters sent in the mid-sixteenth century by a Genoese merchant, Giovanni Francesco di Negro. In one, he wrote, "I urge and implore you not to put much of your money in the hands of strangers and less in those in whom you do not have faith, because as you can see every hour there are new bankruptcies" (Court, 2014: 106). Given that merchant ledgers remained secret, the solvency of a business remained a mystery, and trust took on great importance. For that reason, di Negro wrote, "I am pleased that you persist in the service of those gentlemen to their satisfaction because getting good experience in that business will [earn] you honor and profit" (Court, 2014: 92). In modern terms, the trust established by strong ties facilitated future transactions.

If participants with weak ties were embedded in a network of ties, and if their networks overlapped significantly – perhaps due to family connections, common friends, geographic proximity, or related commercial activities – then this crisscrossing of engagement and information flow could create levels of trust as powerful as strong ties (Granovetter, 1973). That crisscross was the norm for transactions conducted in a city the size of Florence, and certainly in smaller ones. There were few degrees of separation between wealthy and less successful members of the same extended family (Herlihy and Klapisch-Zuber, 1985). In Italy, and especially in Tuscany, numerous scholars have focused on the many ties that bind kin, friends, and neighbors.[5] Naturally, this weave of trust extended into the art world, at least for most patrons. In contrast, when Italian non-elites, often shopkeepers and peasants, left provisions for art commissions in their last wills and testaments, typically decorations for a church, convent, or hospital, they almost never mentioned specific artists (Cohn, 2021: 43). Most probably, their circle of kin, friends, and neighbors did not include many painters. Instead, non-elites put their trust in the ecclesiastical institutions that were obliged to fulfill the legal obligations of wills to commission works of art.

Strong ties facilitated some of the most famed transactions for commissioned art. However, weak ties played a facilitating role in many Renaissance art transactions when strong ties did not exist between critical parties. The prime requirement was that sufficient information flowed about past performance to shape future expectations about adequate performance. "Reputational externalities," a new concept to scholars, added to weak ties and overlapping networks to foster information flow. Reputational externalities describe how trust travels across a group of individuals who possess similar characteristics.[6] For example, good experience with one doctor, one cloth merchant, or one artist will lead you to think more highly of others in these professions, and conversely with a bad experience. If patrons learned in general that artists were tardy, they would expect their artists to be tardy. The information from reputational externalities is less reliable than the information from direct experience. Nevertheless, it is important because it is much more abundant. And when the uniting characteristic between individuals is membership in a selective organization, such as an artists' guild, then the reputational information is much stronger. As we will see in Section 5, such organizations have powerful motivations to demand high quality among their members.

---

[5] This approach was pioneered in a 1976 article by Christiane Klapisch-Zuber, translated in Klapisch-Zuber (1986), followed by F. W. Kent and Dale Kent. For an introduction, as well as many recent studies, see Howard and Hewlett (2016); for its application to art patronage, see Kent (2000) and Eckstein (2010).

[6] This concept, discussed by Richard Zeckhauser in classroom lectures since the 1990s, has not been previously published, and will be addressed in a forthcoming article in an economics journal.

In the absence of strong ties, three elements enabled extensive communication flows: weak ties, significant network overlap, and reputational externalities. These flows were one of the three components that enabled art transactions to go forward. Trust and social capital were the other two components. Trust was basically the expectation that each party to a transaction would behave as if a firm, enforceable contract had been signed, and performance was readily monitored. Thus, artists would not pass off excessive work to assistants, dealers would accurately describe a work, and patrons or buyers would not chisel on an agreed payment.

Social capital refers to the benefits a society, or a group within it, gains from the network of relationships that promote shared values, trust, and cooperation. Tighter groups usually enjoy more social capital. In an innovative analysis of the Brancacci Chapel in the Florentine church of Santa Maria del Carmine, Nicholas Eckstein explores the formal and informal bonds of community among fifteenth-century artists and their clients (Eckstein, 2010). He focuses on one Florentine neighborhood and the levels of cooperation within it. The lesson, however, is general: social capital greased the wheels of the art business across Renaissance Europe. The term social capital was first defined a century ago, and the concept has since been elaborated and debated by numerous distinguished scholars, including sociologists Pierre Bourdieu and James Coleman, political scientist Robert Putnam, and urbanist Jane Jacobs (Eckstein and Terpstra, 2010).

Our trio of concepts – extensive communication flows, trust, and social capital – are strongly interlinked. Each reinforced the other in a virtuous triangle, as shown by the arrows flying in both directions in Figure 5. The arrows – dotted from extensive communication flows, dashed from social capital, and dot-dashed from trust – represent these bolstering forces. Triangles constitute the strongest shape. However, if the sides are not sturdy and secure, a transaction will be risky. One, or conceivably both, parties can get hurt. The flying arrows sometimes miss their target. When they do, trust may be lost; reliability may be diminished. Errant arrows enable the risks that produce the litany of losses described in this volume. In the Renaissance art world, this three-component triangle created a reasonably sturdy structure for taming risk. Thus, a significant division of labor was enabled, which in turn provided a broad array of goods on an efficient basis. The widespread production and sale of skilled artworks certainly required both a division of labor and significant risk taming.

As we indicate throughout this volume, commissioned art presented more transaction risk than most goods. There were frequent delays between initiating and completing a transaction. The product was almost always individualized, implying that information flows along networks would be less informative. There were significant concerns for quality and dignity. Finally, a buyer might

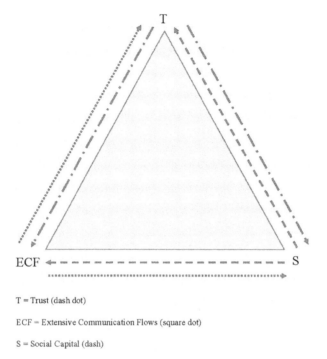

T = Trust (dash dot)

ECF = Extensive Communication Flows (square dot)

S = Social Capital (dash)

Figure 5 Enabling trust.

chisel, and a completed work oriented to a patron, such as a portrait or an altarpiece depicting unusual saints, could be very hard to resell. All these characteristics magnified risks.

The major benefit of trust was risk reduction. It made a negative outcome from purchasing or commissioning a work less likely. Thus, given trust, those who wanted or needed paintings and sculptures were much more willing to purchase or commission them. As the art world grew in volume and geographic spread, patrons and buyers turned increasingly to artists, dealers, and other intermediaries they did not know well. Many came from different cities, regions, or countries. Already in the eleventh century, as discussed in a study widely cited by economists, reputations played a major role in the coalitions of Maghribi traders around the Mediterranean (Greif, 1989).

Such distant transactions raised the potential for negative outcomes, as Duke Ferdinando de' Medici in Florence learned in 1588. He commissioned a bronze frame for the Holy Sepulcher in Jerusalem. Unfortunately, when the expensive gift arrived in this distant land, it turned out to be too small (Ronen, 1970: 432). Artists creating custom-made works for distant settings had to trust intermediaries for essential information such as measurements. When that trust proved misplaced, disaster ensued. Sometimes, this failure of trust resulted from incompetence; in other cases, someone violated trust to obtain an advantage. Trust could only reduce risks; it could not eliminate them. Participants in the international art world found these trust-trimmed risks acceptable given the accompanying benefits. Alternatives were often few or nonexistent. For example, commissions remained the only way to obtain a portrait, and, for most Italian artists through the sixteenth century, patronage provided the sole means to sell major paintings and sculptures.

Anthony Pym's "Translating as Risk Management" (2015) provides a rare study that applies risk analysis to cultural productions. Two of his categories aptly apply to Renaissance art. "Communicative risk" refers to the way texts are interpreted and used in contexts. Much as a translator might misunderstand the meaning or nuance of a source text, artists might misconstrue a patron's request or misinterpret the story the patron selected for representation. The less one understands the culture that produced a source text, the greater the risk of mistranslation. If, say, a patron asks a local artist to produce a scene that is standard for their society, the communicative risks are low. For this reason, most Renaissance contracts for art specified little about the subject beyond the most basic description, such as a list of figures to represent, or a popular narrative, such as the Annunciation. Communicative risks increase when artists are requested to depict unusual subjects or obscure individuals. In those cases, contracts often provide details (Gilbert, 1998). For example, sculptures made north of the Alps often depict the dead Christ in the lap of his mother, but this subject was much less common in Italy. Thus, when a French cardinal commissioned Michelangelo to depict a marble version for his tomb in the basilica of St. Peter's Rome, he included a definition of the term "pietà." For this work, the patron (or his intermediaries) did communicate with the artist and, we assume, approved preliminary plans.

In his article, Pym also refers to a "credibility risk," which might be considered less than full trust between key players involved in a translation or in the final product itself. Andrea Rizzi, Birgit Lang, and Pym develop the credibility risk concept in their book, *What Is Translation History? A Trust-Based Approach* (2019). Among potential risks, they consider how "publishers and clients lose money from poorly performed and produced translations ... Translators also risk their reputations every time they accept a job. From the perspective of the end user, clients accept the risk that the texts they paid for may not be reliable" (Rizzi, Lang, and Pym, 2019: 12). Change the subject of the sentence to Renaissance art, and the passage applies directly. So too does the authors' sustained consideration of how the translator might (dis)trust the patron or client, and vice versa.

In an influential article, Luhmann states that "trust is a solution to a specific problem of risk" (Luhmann, 1988: 95). He discusses how the very appearance of the term "risk" in the early modern period indicates the possibility of unexpected and undesirable results flowing from a decision. Thus, you have the option of commissioning a painting from a little-known artist, today's equivalent of buying a used car. In either case, you might be dissatisfied. "If you choose one action in preference to others in spite of the possibility of being disappointed by the action of others, you define the situation as one of trust" (Luhmann, 1988: 97). In sixteenth-century Italy, when international and transcontinental commerce constituted a significant portion of the economy, "correspondents were frequently far distant and beyond surveillance. As a result, interpersonal trust became fundamental to the operation of the Renaissance economy" (Baker, 2021: 74).

Misrepresentation and Materials

Deliberate misrepresentation sits at the apex of credibility risk in the world of Renaissance art. Many accounts document the falsification of ancient works, which were far more expensive than modern ones (Kurz, 1948). In the late sixteenth century, both Vasari and Van Mander wrote as well about forgeries of contemporary art, specifically engravings that imitated works by Albrecht Dürer. The production and sale of these works undermined trust; their existence imposed a range of risks for the buyers, forgers, and the original artist. Dürer even wrote at the end of his woodcut series of *The Life of the Virgin*: "Woe to you! You thieves and imitators of other people's labor and talents" (Kurz, 1948: 106). For Dürer, the most famous of Germany's artists, forgeries created a credibility risk. Buyers beware!

The repercussions of forgeries stretched far. Van Mander (1994: 301) recounts that Hans Bol decided "to abandon canvas painting entirely when he saw that his canvases were bought and copied on a large scale and sold as if they were his. In turn, he devoted himself totally to painting landscapes and small histories in miniature saying: 'Now let them labor in vain trying to copy me in this.'" Bol's contemporaries interpreted his decision to make miniatures, some still extant, as his response to the unusual production risk of fraudulent imitation by others.

Far more often, patrons and buyers obtained works presented as creations by the master artist but created in part by his workshop. This standard procedure served to both save time and train apprentices. Naturally, this led to a range in quality, as surviving documents make clear. Pantoja de la Cruz, the principal portrait artist at the Spanish court at the turn of the sixteenth century, received 4,000 reals for one painting of Queen Margaret of Austria but only 100 for another. The first was a gift for the king of England; the second, presumably by the workshop, was for a nobleman (Falomir, 2006: 140). Sometimes, paintings or

Figure 6 Domenico Ghirlandaio and workshop, *Rimini altarpiece*, 1493–96, tempera and oil on panel, Museo della Città "L. Tonini," Rimini.
Photo: Courtesy of the Museo della Città "L. Tonini," Rimini.

sculptures were made entirely by the workshop but passed off as a product of the master. When such misrepresentations were detected, patrons typically withheld payment, often with the support of the legal system. For example, soon after Elisabetta Aldobrandini commissioned an altarpiece from Domenico Ghirlandaio, the artist died in 1493 (Figure 6). The patron, dissatisfied with the completed piece, refused to make the final payment. The case went to court. Remarkably, we have the report of the arbitrator; he cited expert opinions that the painting was carried out poorly by students less skilled than the master. Not surprisingly, the court sided with the patron (Nelson and Zeckhauser, 2021: 19–20). In a similar vein, the town council of Brescia objected in 1568 that one of the ceiling canvases they had commissioned from Titian was not painted by him and refused to pay the full amount (Piazza, 2018). In both cases, the patron trusted the artist to produce a work largely "by his own hand," a legal formula included in many contracts. According to Vasari (1912–15, 5: 153), Perino del Vaga received a commission to paint frescoes in the palace of the ruling Doria family in Genoa but had some of the work carried out by Pordenone. When Prince Andrea detected the difference between the two parts, he fired Perino and hired a third painter, Domenico Beccafumi. Most objections to excessive workshop assistance or subcontracting arose from dissatisfaction with the quality of the finished work.

We can consider the negative outcome to be a blend of production and reception risk. Several examples get attention in Section 3.

Misrepresentations of materials represent a credibility risk of a different type. Across Europe, contracts and guild regulations regularly specified the required quality of both pigments and metals, especially gold and silver (Kirby, 2000). These documents prohibit substituting a poorer quality material for a better one. Patrons, buyers, and reputable artists undoubtedly feared that all that glittered was not gold. Technical analysis confirms that Gentile da Fabriano mixed various impurities into the gold he used for his Valle Romita polyptych, and this is probably true for many other works (McCall, 2018: 260).

In some cases, at least, the use of "impure" materials represented more misunderstandings between patrons and artists, rather than misrepresentations. Wealthy patrons – often having little technical expertise – wanted the most illustrious and expensive materials used. Artists, having technical knowledge, would have known how to properly mix and manipulate materials for the best effect, but not necessarily requiring the highest quality or cost of materials.[7] But deception could pay, and artists and merchants did take advantage. In the mid-sixteenth century, when collectors across Europe looked for examples of feather mosaics produced in modern-day Mexico, they were at risk of receiving fakes. They could have read in Bernardino de Sahagun's *Florentine codex* about the "fraudulent embellisher of feathers" who "sells old, worn feathers, damaged feathers; he dyes those which are faded, dirty, yellow, darkened, smoked" (Russo, 2011: 392).

A step beyond fraud was filching. Patrons had to be on guard against the theft of materials, and precious ones were particularly at risk. In Rome, Pope Paul V gave the nobleman Pier Vincenzo Strozzi responsibility to oversee the renovation of the Cappella Paolina in the church Santa Maria Maggiore. Strozzi, it seems, stole some lapis lazuli purchased for that project. He then gave it to the artist Antonio Tempesta and commissioned him to use it in another painting, *Pearl Fishing* unrelated to the chapel (Figure 7) (Nygren, 2021: 136). Every link in the supply chain required trust. Thus, artists and artisans had to trust the merchants who sold them materials. Few tests seeking to distinguish most true jewels, metals, and pigments from cheaper imitations were reliable. Hence, purchasers had to rely on their eyes and especially the reputations of the sellers. Some materials presented particular risks to artists, quite apart from intentional misrepresentation. Large blocks of marble, for example, often contained flaws or long colored lines, known as veins, made by deposits of crystalized minerals. When carving a *Standing Christ* in white marble, Michelangelo

---

[7] We thank Sharifa Lookman for this observation, and the one below about repurposed bronze.

Figure 7 Antonio Tempesta, *Pearl Fishing*, ca. 1610, oil on lapis lazuli, Musée du Louvre, Paris. Photo: RMN-Grand Palais / Art Resource, NY.

discovered a black vein. As a result, he had to abandon the block and start a second version. Costs for the piece escalated, as did delays (Carlson, 2021).

Patrons and buyers relied on and trusted artists to use the soundest practices when securing, using, or shipping materials and works. Reliance sometimes failed, perhaps to save costs, but ignorance or sloppiness also contributed. In a letter, King Philip II of Spain complained because a very visible crease disfigured Titian's *Venus and Adonis* (Madrid; Figure 8). The canvas painting had been folded for shipping, but the safe practice was to roll it on a pole. According to Vasari, Perugino did not use oil paint properly. As a result, some of his paintings "have suffered considerably, and they are all cracked in the dark parts" (Vasari, 1912–15, 5: 38). In a similar vein, Van Mander (1994: 289) wrote that before painting a large canvas, Pieter Pourbus "had primed it too thickly with a glue ground." Moreover, that particular work "was frequently rolled up and rolled out, and so it cracked and flaked off in many places." Michelangelo's lack of skill in bronze casting undermined his first attempt to create a statue of Julius II for the church of San Petronio in Bologna (Hendler, 2021). His second casting proved successful, but the piece suffered a different fate. Just a few years later, a revolution in Bologna overthrew the ruling Bentivoglio family, and the bronze sculpture was melted down. The risk of this dramatic outcome was enhanced because the sculpture's material was expensive and easily recyclable.

Figure 8 Titian, *Venus and Adonis*, 1554, oil on canvas, Museo Nacional del Prado, Madrid. Photo: Wikimedia.

Repurposed bronze for a new statue brought production risks to an artist. It was impossible to determine the precise combination of metals used to create the bronze. This introduced a wide array of unknowns, including the melting point, porosity, and fracture of the metal, catalysts for catastrophe in the finicky chemistry of casting.

Financial Risks

When artists produced quality works, they trusted patrons to pay them the agreed sum. This compensation was often stipulated in registered contracts for altarpieces and fresco cycles. For other works, payment was usually the subject of private agreements. On very rare occasions, a stingy patron could be taken to court, as happened with Elisabetta Aldobrandini, though she won the case. But artists had other weapons for extracting payment or taking revenge on short-changing patrons, as we learn from Van Mander and Vasari. Their well-known publications alerted readers to the financial risks faced by artists. Van Mander recounts two amusing tales, perhaps fabricated, about Flemish painters working for foreigners. The first concerns the portrait of an English captain by Jacques de Poindre (or Jacob de Punder). The captain, Pieter Andries, abandoned the work without paying. De Punder reputedly added "bars in watercolor in front of the face so that it appeared as though the captain was in prison and put it on display" (Van Mander, 1994: 187). In a similar vein, Gillis Mostaert painted an image of the Virgin for a Spaniard, but when he did not receive adequate compensation "he covered it with an undercoat of chalk and glue on which he painted Mary wildly decked-out and as flippant as a whore" (Van Mander, 1994: 302). In the end, both painters got paid and removed the offending additions. Vasari tells more plausible stories about artists who refused to consign works for payment considered insufficient, such as Tribolo's sculpted angel for the Pisa Cathedral (Vasari, 1912–15, 7:7). Sodoma, we read, did not complete a painting cycle in Siena in part because of his own "caprice, and partly because he had not been paid" (Vasari, 1912–15, 7: 254). When Michelangelo sent Angelo Doni his painting of the *Holy Family* (Florence; Figure 9), he requested the reasonable compensation of 70 ducats. The miserly merchant tried to pay merely 40. Offended, the artist reputedly demanded and received double the original price (Vasari, 1912–15, 9: 19).

In three dramatic passages, Vasari recounts how the sculptors Donatello, Pietro Torrigiani, and Matteo dal Nassaro took the extreme step of destroying their work rather than selling it for less than it was worth (Vasari, 1912–15, 2: 245; 4:187; 5:377). More often, we can assume, an "underpaid" artist tried to

Figure 9 Michelangelo, *Doni Tondo*, 1505–1506, tempera grassa on panel, Gallerie degli Uffizi, Florence. Photo: Wikimedia.

sell his work to someone who would pay more, as did the painter Bartholomeus Spranger (Van Mander, 1994: 341). Naturally, the new owner might have different needs. Thus, when Francesco Torbido failed to receive payment for a portrait of a Venetian gentleman, "he had the Venetian dress changed into that of a shepherd" and recycled the painting to a certain Monsignor de Martini (Vasari, 1912–15, 6: 25). Who knows how many commissioned works changed appearance or owners because artists found ways to mitigate their most important production risk? In addition, an artist's potential refusal to sell was a threat that helped deter patrons who might otherwise haggle about the price.

Some disputes ultimately led to happier endings. Andrea del Sarto's celebrated fresco cycle depicting the *Life of San Filippo* (Figure 10), for the Florentine church of the Santissima Annunziata, was one. With reduced compensation offered, the painter refused to finish the cycle. The patron "would not release him from his bond without Andrea first promising that he would paint two other scenes, at his own leisure and convenience." In the end, the artist received "an increase of payment, and thus they came to terms" (Vasari, 1912–15, 5: 90).

Figure 10 Andrea del Sarto, *Death of Saint Philip Benizi and Resurrection of a Child,* 1510, fresco, Santissima Annunziata, Florence. Photo: Wikimedia.

Trust was at the center of the Renaissance art business, but many untrustworthy participants operated at the periphery. Thus, some patrons underpaid. Some artists created substandard works. Some outlier artists even engaged in nefarious financial practices. In 1596, the Art Academy of Rome took action. For example, it established regulations to prohibit artists from underbidding for a commission already entrusted to another. In 1607, the Academy introduced penalties for artists who obtained a commission with a low bid and then increased the price as the work progressed (Cavazzini, 2008: 168–9). To justify these new rules, both activities must have been widespread in Rome and presumably elsewhere.

Naturally, many types of financial risks emerged that did not involve trust. As Larry Silver discusses in Section 4, open markets, first in Antwerp and then across Europe, encouraged artists to specialize in genre paintings. When the fashion for these dimmed, prices fell. Many players beyond the artists themselves needed to predict the movement of the marketplace. A series of letters from 1665 evinces how Balthasar Moretus II, an important Belgian printer and publisher, dealt with financial risks in the ornate book trade. If Cornelis de Wael, an artist and dealer, wanted to undertake sales at his own risk, he would receive a 25 percent discount on the price plus a 5 percent commission; alternatively, the publisher would assume the risk but offer no discount and a lower commission (Stoesser, 2018: 71).

Delivery Risks

The most frequent risk for art commissions was delay or non-completion. Numerous accounts report patrons frustrated over delays. Francesco del Giocondo never received the portrait he commissioned of his wife, (Mona) Lisa, which wound up in the hands of French king François I. Worse yet, perhaps, Leonardo and his workshop made nude variations of the painting (Nelson and Zeckhauser, 2021). In his discussion of Parmigianino's frescoes in the church of the Steccata, Parma, Vasari (5: 251–2) wrote that the artist began to "carry it on so slowly that it was evident that he was not in earnest . . . the Company of the Steccata, perceiving that he had completely abandoned the work . . . brought a suit against him." Surviving records confirm that Parmigianino worked on frescoes in the Steccata (Figure 11) on and off between 1533 and 1539 (Ekserdjian, 2006: 10). He never completed the cycle.

In 1478, the Augustinian canons at the convent of San Donato a Scopeto, just outside the walls of Florence, took a calculated risk when they commissioned Leonardo da Vinci to paint the *Adoration of the Magi* for the high altar. He had never produced a large-scale painting for anyone, though the painter had received a commission for an altarpiece in the town hall. Nevertheless, Leonardo was the

Figure 11 Parmigianino, *Three Foolish Virgins* (detail), 1530s, fresco, Santa Maria della Steccata, Parma. Photo: Wikimedia.

son of a notary who often worked for the convent; that boosted confidence for the patrons. Ultimately, the canons stipulated a contract with Leonardo that addressed their concerns about delay or non-completion (Bambach, 2019, 1:242–43). The canons hedged their bets through both requirements and financial arrangements. To begin with, Leonardo had to work on the commission for four months before the patron made a formal agreement. During this time, most probably, the artist had to provide finished drawings, or perhaps even the underpaint, still visible on the wooden panel today. Two additional clauses in the contract were designed to encourage Leonardo to complete the work within the stipulated two-year period. The artist would have to pay for all his materials, and he would lose all rights to the panel if it remained unfinished. These risk-reducing arrangements proved insufficient. Leonardo departed Florence for better opportunities in Milan in 1482, leaving the altarpiece started but never completed.

Contract provisions that incorporated punishments for delays were one tool to help patrons avoid tardy deliveries. Advisors, who informed patrons about artistic quality, were a second. Letters from 1663 to Don Antonio Ruffo, Prince of Scaletta, indicate that Cornelis de Wael warned him against ordering a painting by Claude Lorrain, a slow worker, or from Nicolas Poussin, as he was too frail (Stoesser, 2018: 82). This rare documentation provides insight into the advisory roles intermediaries played between countless patrons and artists. "Rather than being a 'two-way' street, the process of art patronage," as Sheryl Reiss noted, "was, in fact, a complicated 'multi-lane highway', often involving intermediaries" (Reiss, 2013: 26). These middlemen often served to reduce the risk of disappointment for patrons.

A few major Renaissance artists often left commissions unfinished, but what did their contemporaries make of this behavior? We find some clues in the short biographies of Leonardo, Michelangelo, and others written by the humanist Paolo Giovio in about 1525 (Nelson and Zeckhauser, 2018). Giovio observed that Leonardo completed very few of the many commissions he received. He was unstable in character and readily lost interest in his works. This assessment would sour the enthusiasm of many a potential patron. Michelangelo proved even less reliable than Leonardo. Giovio noted that Michelangelo was commissioned to build the tomb of Pope Julius II and, having received many thousands of gold florins, he made several very large statues. What Giovio left unsaid – but what everyone in Rome knew – was that the tomb, two decades after its commission, remained unfinished. It was later completed, with major sections carried out by assistants, including the recumbent image of the pope himself. Even the most famous artists could be unreliable, some frequently so, and yet, despite the significant risks, major commissions still came their way. Patrons felt the risks were worth it given that the upside was art by the biggest names of the day.

Cardinal Giulio de' Medici, cousin to Pope Leo X, offered extremely generous compensation when he commissioned an altarpiece from Michelangelo's friend Sebastiano (Nelson and Zeckhauser, 2018: 18). Payment for Sebastiano's *Raising of Lazarus* (London) (Figure 12) was estimated to be about 850 florins. To put that figure in context, Michelle O'Malley's fundamental study of art commissions in Renaissance Italy, based on nearly 250 documented paintings, established that almost two-thirds of the altarpieces commissioned before 1600 cost one hundred florins or less (O'Malley, 2005: 133). A full 85 percent of such works cost under two hundred florins. Giulio probably expected that the artist would drop his other work in progress and begin the altarpiece, and Sebastiano did just that. (Economists refer to this phenomenon as "efficiency wages": employers pay above market rates to encourage workers to be unusually diligent or honest.) In 1516 Giulio also commissioned Raphael's *Transfiguration* (Figure 13), which cost at least as much as Sebastiano's altarpiece. Here too, extraordinary compensation functioned as a risk-management tool. It reduced

Figure 12 Sebastiano del Piombo, The *Raising of Lazarus,* 1517–1519, oil on
panel, The National Gallery, London. Photo: Wikimedia.

the possibility that the commissioned work would arrive late or not at all. In
seventeenth-century Bologna, and presumably elsewhere, patrons employed
still another risk-management instrument. Established artists were often given
advance payments to help ensure that they would accept and complete commissions. No risk-management instrument offers perfect security and this one
sometimes failed. For example, Guido Reni was so popular and overbooked
that he returned many cash advances rather than undertake the contracted work
(Morselli, 2010: 162).

Cardinal Giulio had to wait four years for Raphael's *Transfiguration*, given
the competition for the famous artist's time from other major patrons of
architectural projects, fresco cycles, and large independent paintings. Three of
the latter had been ordered by someone even more important than the cardinal:
his cousin Pope Leo. Two altarpieces, now in Paris and made in collaboration
with Raphael's workshop, served as papal gifts for the king of France. The third

Figure 13 Raphael, *Transfiguration,* 1516–1520, tempera grassa on panel, Musei Vaticani, Vatican City. Photo: Wikimedia.

painting was Raphael's celebrated group portrait, now in Florence, which includes both Leo and Giulio. Big spending Giulio could be reasonably confident that his commissioned masterpiece would arrive, and very confident that it would be well received. His confidence was justified. As we explore in the next section, scores of other Renaissance works fared less well.

3 Reception Risks: Inappropriate Iconography and Substandard Skill

Renaissance sources make relatively few allusions to production problems in art. In contrast, a plethora of artistic treatises, letters, poems, biographies, and archival documents from the late fifteenth through the early seventeenth centuries provide an abundance of evidence of paintings and sculptures being poorly received. Indeed, an entire literary genre, vituperative poems, grew up in Italy during this period. These poems were inspired by ancient Greek epigrams that ridiculed artists and their works (Gamberini, 2021; Spagnolo, 2021). These comedic texts seriously threatened the reputations of patrons, owners, and especially artists. The varied goals of these players, be it to increase fame, display status, convey a message, or adorn a setting, got trampled when their art was harshly attacked, whether by words or actions.

Filippo Strozzi, a wealthy Florentine banker, contemplated reception risks when he wrote to his brother in 1477 about plans for a family tomb: "Things like this, done for honor, should be such that they induce that response, because otherwise one only gets shame from them" (Borsook, 1970: 15 n. 17). Such dishonor might result from the criticism of expert viewers, including artists. Sometimes, artists even worked together to dampen the likelihood of criticism by other contemporaries. The 1607 statutes of the Art Academy in Rome, to which all major artists belonged, prohibited membership to anyone who "made or had made, either published or in manuscript, texts that criticized the reputation of Academy professors" (Cavazzini, 2008: 44). Criticism could be costly, and severe punishments could deter it.

We distinguish between two main categories of reception risks: inappropriate iconography and substandard skill. These roughly correspond to problems in content and in form, with some overlap. As an example of the former, theologians across Early Modern Europe debated the responsibility of artists who created "sinful" portraits that facilitated illicit relationships (Schwartz, 2019: 100–18). Both content and form were in play for Baccio Valori, who reaped more shame than honor when he decorated the façade of his Florentine home with a series of expensive marble portraits. To his dismay, they were ridiculed for having ugly visages, or *visacci*, thus giving his home its nickname of the Palazzo dei Visacci (Williams, 1993) (Figure 14). The sculptor, as creator of these ostensibly ugly pieces, was blasted as well. More damaging for Valori than the damning sobriquet for his abode were sonnets written by his learned contemporaries lampooning the patron for mixing genres and having portraits placed on herms. Some objected to images of citizens publicly "impaled," a clear violation of premodern decorum.

In religious art, details that violated theological beliefs or more often, the rules of decorum got denounced. Sometimes, the patrons voiced their decorum concerns after seeing preparatory drawings, an essential phase in the production of Renaissance art and one that helped avoid reception risks. For example, Pope Clement VIII commissioned Federico Barocci in 1603 to paint an altarpiece depicting the *Institution of the Eucharist*, for the church of Santa Maria sopra Minerva in Rome. According to Giovanni Bellori's account, published in 1672,

Figure 14 Giovanni Battista Caccini, *Palazzo dei Visacci* (detail), 1593–1604, marble, Palazzo dei Visacci, Florence. Photo: Wikimedia.

the patron asked to see a preparatory drawing. Having viewed it, he instructed the painter to remove the representation of the Devil. This story is supported by the presence of the satanic figure in an extant drawing (Ekserdjian, 2021: 37). Writing in Northern Europe, Erasmus of Rotterdam also condemned the violation of decorum in religious works: "Some artists, when they paint something from the Evangelists add impious absurdities to it . . . although these things are blasphemous and impious, they still pass for humor" (Kaplan, 1997: 101–2). The Catholic reformer described genre scenes in the background of religious scenes, and he was not amused.

Sometimes, the reasons for rejecting preliminary plans were stylistic, as we read in Vasari's account of Giovann'Antonio Sogliani's fresco in the refectory of the Dominican convent of San Marco in Florence. The friars rejected the first project, known to us and them from drawings. They found it too busy, and wanted things "positive, ordinary, and simple." The simplified style of Sogliani's second version, still visible at San Marco, met these requirements perfectly.

Churchmen, from Girolamo Savonarola in the late fifteenth century to the participants at the Council of Trent, which ended in 1563, also objected to art that they deemed too complicated and complex. Such intricacy highlighted the skill of the artist, raising the danger that the religious content would be over-shadowed or distorted. The clearest and best-known expression of this press for simplicity appeared in Giovanni Gilio's *Dialogue on the Errors and Abuses of Painters* (1564) which criticized many works for their excess of recondite details and learned allusions and their contorted figures (Maffei, 2017). Gilio pointed to the errors and abuses found in Michelangelo's *Last Judgment*, including excessive nudity (Figure 15). The objection was not merely content; Giovio also objected to Michelangelo putting his skill on display. He asserted that Michelangelo included nude figures to demonstrate his ingenuity and

Figure 15 Michelangelo, *Christ* (detail of *The Last Judgment*), 1534–41, fresco, Sistine Chapel, Vatican City. Photo: Wikimedia.

anatomical knowledge. Similarly, Vasari's life of Fra Bartolomeo recounts an unwarranted display of skill. For the Florentine church of San Marco, Fra Bartolomeo painted a highly praised "St Sebastian, naked, very lifelike in the coloring of the flesh, sweet in countenance, and likewise executed with corresponding beauty of person." During confessions, however, friars learned about "women who had sinned at the sight of it, on account of the charm and melting beauty of the lifelike reality" (Vasari, 1912–15, 6: 158). In both works, the artist's skill, as well as the content, rendered the nude figures unacceptable.

When viewers and patrons objected to the appearance of a painting or sculpture, the written record rarely reveals whether the concern was that the artist chose an inappropriate style, lacked ability, had an off day, worked too fast, or delegated excessively to workshop assistants. We group these disparate problems in the category of "substandard skill." Vasari reports that several Florentine artists wrote sonnets criticizing Perugino because he recycled several figures found in earlier paintings. Vasari deplored his poverty of imagination (Nelson, 2004). Vituperative poems, especially those attacking an individual artist, were usually more explicit, pointing to straightforward deficiencies of pictorial skills, such as distorted proportions and inaccurate anatomies.

In *Macaronea*, for example, readers in the late Quattrocento learned that the unhappy patrons of Canziano sued the painter frequently and with good reason: his chickens looked like horses and his men like wooden mannequins (Gamberini, 2021: 76, 80). In his depictions of the Madonna and Child, viewers could not even distinguish one from the other. These laughable errors bring us back to Gilio, who warned that artists must avoid derision if their works are to teach and arouse devotion. For a German artist's perspective, we turn again to Albrecht Dürer. His treatise explained that, in the past, his countrymen made works revealing their ignorance about proportions and the rules of art. "Whenever knowledgeable painters and true masters saw such unconsidered work, they laughed at the blindness of these people, and not unfairly so, since nothing is less pleasing to a man of good sense than mistakes in painting" (Gombrich, 1976: 112). Comparable errors were noted in a tract dedicated to sculpture (1504) by the Paduan humanist Pomponio Gaurico. He attacked those Tuscans who exaggerated the musculature of figures in action. Gaurico noted that Verrocchio made the horse in his Colleoni equestrian monument (Venice) "in such a crudely realistic fashion that the animal appears to be flayed" (Campbell, 2019: 16). Michelangelo was verbally flayed, not infrequently, for the excessive hardness of the muscles he portrayed (Nelson, 2002). Titian was criticized for depicting the angel Gabriel in his 1562 Naples *Annunciation* as too plump. We learn this from a defense of the painting written the same year by Bartolomeo Maranta, a learned physician, who explained that the angel's fleshy body corresponds to that of a sanguine person

Figure 16 Giovan Francesco Caroto, *Three Archangels*, ca. 1500–55, oil on canvas, Museo degli Affreschi, Verona. Photo: Wikimedia.

(Freedman, 2015: 25). Some artists evidently had problems in creating the appropriate body type for angels. Writing about Giovan Francesco Caroto's *Three Archangels* (Figure 16), Vasari reported (1912–15, 6: 16) that the North Italian painter was reproached "for having made the legs of those Angels too slender and wanting in softness." Writing about another work, Vasari (1912–15, 6: 19) informs us that Caroto was "told by a priest that his figures were too seductive for altarpieces" (Gaston, 1995: 243 n. 12). For this churchman, the use of an inappropriate style probably indicated a lack of skill since artists were expected to know how soft or seductive a figure should – or shouldn't – be. Of course, a failure in decorum differs significantly from an inability to paint soft legs on an angel or to distinguish between a Madonna and Child. Nevertheless, at times, objections about decorum could be presented or camouflaged as objections to skill.

Failed Communication

Beyond objections to an artist's lack of skill or unwelcome virtuosity, an artist's message might be misinterpreted or deemed inappropriate. We adapt the etic approach examined in an article on "Advertising Gone Wrong." It presented the *Fontana dell'Acqua Felice* in Rome (Figure 17), commissioned by Pope Sixtus V,

Figure 17 Prospero Bresciano, *Fontana dell'Acqua Felice*, 1587–1588, marble, Largo di Santa Susanna, Rome. Photo: Wikimedia.

as a "failed communication channel" (Cholcman and Maharshak, 2014). The authors tweak an analytic framework, initially created to evaluate advertisements, to explore how public art conveys a message, and how such conveyance could go astray. For three key concepts used in advertising – image, headline, and text – the authors propose parallels in art on public display: visibility, central message, and elaboration. A prime source of risks for both advertising and public art is what the authors label "noise" to indicate elements that distract from or disrupt the main message. (We prefer the term "interference.") From the perspective of the critics quoted above, interference can result from overly sensuous or realistic nudes, excessively muscular or stiff figures, the inappropriate appearance of the Devil, or incomprehensible representations of chickens and Madonnas.

Located at the end of the first modern aqueduct bringing water to Rome, the *Fontana dell'Acqua Felice* celebrated the patron, Pope Sixtus V, through its imposing size and highly visible placement. Moreover, a series of other figures, reliefs, and inscriptions elaborated on the main message. But soon after the fountain was unveiled in 1590, one vituperative poem criticized the central figure of Moses as a "monster"; another stated that the unnamed sculptor (Prospero Bresciano) "had lost his mind." Three published texts from the 1600s clarify that the sculpture was considered poorly proportioned, a view shared by viewers ever since (Ostrow, 2006). This criticism of the Moses statue distracted viewers from the central message of the fountain.

The risk that art might mangle messaging increased dramatically when the artist and intended audience came from very different cultures. In a letter of 1604 from the Duke of Florence to his ambassador at the Spanish court concerning a proposed gift of a bronze equestrian monument to King Philip IV, Ferdinando de' Medici observed that it would be a good idea "to understand well the wishes of the King, since it will cost very much money, and then, if he didn't like it, it wouldn't be worth anything" (Helmstutler di Dio, 2015: 181). The Duke, keenly aware of transport issues and risks, also noted that "it might be necessary to make it in several pieces and then have it put together on site." This procedure was in fact followed. Pietro Tacca's *King Philip IV* (Madrid) (Figure 18), the first equestrian monument since antiquity to show a rearing rider, evidently pleased the patron: it was put on display in a prominent location and became a prototype for other sculptors. When it was commissioned, however, Ferdinando recognized that the

Figure 18 Pietro Tacca, *Equestrian Monument of Philip IV*, 1634–40, bronze, Plaza de Oriente, Madrid. Photo: Wikimedia.

innovative monument could easily fail in communication. Like a translator working on a text produced from an unfamiliar society, an artist working for a foreign
audience can easily violate well-established but unwritten rules of decorum. A few
decades later, the Medici court encountered a similar problem when Grand Duke
Ferdinando II sent a painting by Cigoli to Spain as a diplomatic gift, only to have it
rejected as crude and insignificant (Goldberg, 1992). If only the Duke had listened
to his ambassador, a wise intermediary who had strongly recommended against
this proposed gift.

Cross-cultural communication challenges help us understand why the French
court considered Bernini's equestrian portrait of King Louis XIV a failure
(Figure 19). The life-size marble statue, designed by a celebrated foreign artist,
was intended to be prominently displayed in the gardens outside the Palace at
Versailles. Bernini carefully considered his creation. The image of Louis XIV on
a rearing horse was crafted to convey the central message that the French king,
like Philip IV of Spain, was a powerful ruler completely in control of his steed
and, by extension, his realm. According to the biography of Bernini, written by

Figure 19 Gian Lorenzo Bernini, *Equestrian Monument of King Louis XIV*
(transformed by François Girardon into *Marcus Curtius*), 1665–84, marble,
Palace of Versailles, Versailles. Photo: Bridgeman Images.

his son, Domenico, the sculptor elaborated on this theme by showing Louis XIV smiling. In an extended passage, Domenico explained that after a hard-won military victory, "anyone in a state of bliss naturally displays a jubilant expression on his face and an attractive smile on his mouth."

Alas, this feature was criticized by an "intelligent French knight" (Zarucchi, 2013: 369). The unwanted smile must have contributed to Louis XIV's violent negative reaction. Charles Perrault, who helped develop and implement the royal artistic projects, wrote that the sculpture was so hated "that the king had it removed from the spot where it was placed and had the head taken off." The French sculptor François Girardon put on a new head modeled in the classical style. Bernini could have avoided the devastating reception cost had he followed standard procedures designed to reduce production risks. According to Perrault, the Italian sculptor "worked straightaway upon the marble, and did not make a clay model as other sculptors are accustomed to do." Bernini did make a terracotta model, now in Rome, in part because the sculpture was carved by students, but he remained personally responsible for the head. This part of the model shows Louis XIV with a stern expression; evidently, the unusual idea of adding a smile came later. If only Bernini had presented his patron a prototype of the smiling king, he could have adjusted the sculpture's mouth. Instead, major changes in the final work were made by Girardon who, as a professor at the Royal Academy of Painting and Sculpture, surely knew the King's tastes. He even transformed the subject of the portrait into a representation of the ancient Roman hero Marcus Curtius. Stylistic and iconographic innovations, while often welcomed, magnified communication risks.

The more freedom taken by the translator or artist, the more likely the final product will disappoint. For example, King Philip II of Spain wrote a letter in 1551 referring to several portraits by Titian, including a good likeness of himself in armor (Madrid). He noted, however, that Titian made the work too hastily and, had time permitted, the king would have asked the painter to redo the work (Falomir, 2003: 218). This criticism presumably refers to the loose brushstrokes, typical of late works by the Italian painter but unusual in Spain. To this foreign patron, Titian's innovative style communicated excessive haste.

Problematic Portraits

Portraits have particular reception risks since their subjects care greatly about how they are depicted.[8] In the Renaissance, like today, rulers carefully cultivated their images to appear healthy, confident, and powerful. As with King

---

[8] The following paragraphs are based on our essay (Nelson and Zeckhauser, 2021), which includes additional references.

Louis XIV, rulers might even eliminate works that did not fit their goals. A letter from Marquis Ludovico Gonzaga tells us about a portrait drawing by Mantegna that was destroyed. The Marquis of Mantua wrote that, previously, when Mantegna had portrayed the Duke of Milan, "it didn't seem to satisfy him, and we heard he had the sheets of paper burned because he felt Andrea hadn't done him well" (Signorini, 1974: 232). In reply, Ludovico praised his court artist, most faintly: "Andrea is a good master in other things, but in portraits, he could have more grace and doesn't do so well" (Signorini, 1974: 232). In short, the accusation was substandard skill. In the *Camera picta*, Ludovico appears with rolls of fat on his thick neck, a large fleshy ear, and an inelegant pose. The depiction of each feature departed strongly from Renaissance standards of male beauty. Presumably, Ludovico was not pleased.

About twenty years after Ludovico's letter, Isabella d'Este expressed disapproval of Mantegna, seemingly for similar reasons. In 1493, the Marchesa of Mantua wrote that "the painter has done his work so badly that it does not resemble us in the slightest way" (Woods-Marsden, 1987: 210). Turning our modern ideas about skill upside down, Isabella preferred a portrait by Giovanni Santi, an artist of far lesser repute than Mantegna, though she again claimed that the resemblance was poor. Of a third portrait, by yet another artist, she complained that it "is not very much like me because it is a little fatter than I am" (Isabella, 2017: 129). Surely, artists could have created an accurate image of Isabella. Indeed, Ludovico il Moro, the Duke of Milan, even told Isabella that the third portrait "seems to me it resembles you quite well; it is true that it makes you look somewhat fatter than Your Ladyship is, unless you have grown fatter since the last time we saw you" (Dijk, 2015: 123). One portrait did win Isabella's approval. It was painted several years later by Francia, who had never set eyes on the Marchesa. Isabella told the artist, "And since, through your art, you have made us much more beautiful than nature did, we thank you as much as is possible" (Isabella, 2017: 352). But she pushed for a still further enhancement, requesting that the painter make her eyes a bit lighter. Isabella, it seems, disapproved of many portraits because their flattery fell short.

In the sixteenth century, when knowledge about Aristotle's *Poetics* became widespread, many educated patrons surely agreed with his insight that "good portrait painters ... render personal appearance and produce likenesses, yet enhance people's beauty" (Aristotle, 1995: 83, chap. 1454b). As Ferdinando, Duke of Mantua, said of Alessandro Tiarini's portrait of his wife Caterina de' Medici, "You have depicted her better than any other, since you have improved and embellished her looks without diminishing her likeness." In a letter of 1617, she had complained that an earlier portrait had depicted her nose too large

Figure 20 Hans Eworth, *Queen Mary I*, 1554, oil on panel, National Portrait Gallery, London. Photo: National Portrait Gallery, London.

(Bourne, 2007: 231). A portrait's verisimilitude was entwined with the question of its quality. Portraits were required to be a deft blend of accuracy and flattery; tensions were inevitable.

Excessive enhancements brought their own perils, as we can see from the reaction of King Philip II to Hans Eworth's portrait of Mary Tudor (Figure 20). This conforms to period ideals of beauty much more than the austere portrait that Philip later commissioned from Anthonis Mor (Madrid) (Figure 21) (Woodall, 2016: 261–9). Philip first saw Mary in Eworth's idealized work, and according to one ambassador, "the King of Spain had cursed the painters and envoys when he beheld Queen Mary" in person (Von Klarwill, 1928: 218). The gap between art and reality can lead to disappointment.

Part of an artist's skill lay in knowing the mix required for that deft blend between accuracy and flattery, namely, how much to enhance the appearance of a particular individual. Titian's posthumous painting depicting Isabella of Portugal had the widower's advice in the mix (Falomir, 2003: 208–9). Charles V, the Holy Roman emperor, ordered this image of his late wife and asked Titian to work from an earlier painting by a minor artist. In a fascinating letter, the patron asked Titian to retouch the nose, not because the artist had rendered it poorly, but rather because he had painted it accurately. Titian complied and produced an "improvement" on the earlier portrait. Isabel's nose got straightened and idealized. Titian similarly idealized his

Figure 21 Anthonis Mor, *Portrait of Mary Tudor,* 1554, oil on panel, Museo
Nacional del Prado, Madrid. Photo: Wikimedia.

representations of the emperor himself (Figure 22). Charles V displayed an
extremely pronounced version of the so-called Hapsburg jaw. Contemporary
accounts reveal that his chin jutted so far forward that fully closing his mouth
was impossible. However, Titian's many portraits of the ruler reveal not
a trace of the underbite problem that typified his royal line. By contrast,
Christoph Amberger created a portrait of Charles V that veered closer to
reality (Figure 23), to judge from a surviving drawing of the emperor's skull
(Bodart, 2012). Charles evidently preferred the heroic image and going
forward, he gave Titian, not Amberger, the extraordinary honor of being the
only artist permitted to portray him.

  For other patrons, placing inappropriate attributes or symbols in a portrait
could lead to ridicule. In 1584, the artist and writer Giovanni Paolo Lomazzo
wrote that "merchants and bankers who have never seen a drawn sword and who
should probably appear with quill pens behind their ears, their gowns about
them and their day-books in front of them, have themselves painted in armor
holding generals' batons" (Springer, 2010: 162).

Figure 22 Titian, *Emperor Charles V with a Dog*, 1533, oil on canvas, Museo Nacional del Prado, Madrid. Photo: Wikimedia.

Figure 23 Christoph Amberger, *Portrait of Charles V*, ca. 1532, oil on canvas, Gemäldegalerie, Berlin. Photo: Wikimedia.

If portraits were included in larger works, an additional danger arose: the patron and artist had to decide who should be portrayed. In the early fourteenth century, Nello Tolomei, a high government official in the Tuscan city of San Gimignano, decided to adorn the town hall with a frescoed *Maestà*, that is, a Madonna and Child with Saints. Overall, it resembled a famous and slightly earlier version of the *Maestà* by Simone Martini in the nearby city of Siena, but Tolomei's poor judgment was to request the inclusion of a donor portrait. Within twenty years, according to a local chronicler, criticism of the inclusion of the patron's portrait led to a popular revolt (McLean, 2015: 195). About two centuries later, members of the congregation in the Cathedral of Trieste objected to the portrait of the patron Broccardo Malchiostro in the center of Titian's 1520 *Annunciation*. Perhaps the problem was his status as a "foreigner," coming from another city. One cleric stated that the Bishop should have "removed the afore-mentioned image of that mister Broccardo . . . in the middle of the altarpiece. Whoever pulls it down or defaces it will do a good job." Another said, "One will see him defaced with pleasure" (van Kessel, 2017: 110–1). In 1526, perhaps inspired by those comments, an unknown assailant scratched the portrait and smeared it with pitch "and other dirt."

In commissioning a group portrait, as in planning a banquet, the patron faced the difficult decision of whom to invite and, consequently, whom to exclude. The skill of the artist, like that of a modern event organizer, includes the ability to assemble and arrange the guests in a manner that reflected their status. Injured egos were always a risk, and some observers of Mantegna's Court Scene in the *Camera picta*, for example, got theirs bruised. Letters reveal that Duke Galeazzo Maria Sforza, in particular, had expressed his disapproval to the patron, Marquis Ludovico Gonzaga, about being excluded from the gallery of portraits in the frescoes. Ludovico justified his decision, explaining that "the Emperor is my superior, and the King of Denmark is my brother-in-law" (Gilbert, 1992: 131). Most interesting, he added that since these portraits "have been seen by so many people as they have been, it would be too great an awkwardness to remove them." Ludovico claimed to have entertained the possibility of demolishing the two portraits to resolve a diplomatic incident, which suggests that he thought Sforza wanted him to do so. Perhaps the Duke of Milan just wanted his portrait to be added but, in the end, it seems, Ludovico requested no changes.

Reducing the Risks of Bad Reception

When works of art were put on view in the street, church, or public building, as opposed to a private home, the risks of a poor reception ballooned. A "monstrous" fountain could undermine the message of a pope, and an inappropriate tomb might bring shame rather than honor to the patron. In the same spirit, a government official in Prato noted in 1502 that if an altarpiece planned for the town hall "is not excellent, it will bring more dishonor than honor, and, even if obtained with a low cost, it will be completely useless" (O'Malley, 2005: 104). To reduce the risks of bad reception and obtain a useful painting, the patrons had to pay for quality. Doing precisely this, they commissioned a work by their famous native son, Filippino Lippi. This investment paid off because, according to Vasari (1912–15, 4: 4–5), Filippino's altarpiece was highly praised.

Risks to patrons were entwined with those of their artists. The principal-agent model, a prominent concept in such fields as economics and political science, effectively captures that interweaving. Modern lawyers and dressmakers, like Renaissance artists, are agents whose responsibility is to act on behalf of the principals. Once engaged, the agent has substantial latitude, and the principal can only monitor the work in preparation with difficulty, or perhaps not at all. The contracted product is being created from scratch and will only be delivered later, often years after the commission. Quality and an agreed approach may suffer in the interim, due to what decision theorists call "moral hazard." Moral hazard arises when the agent responds to the incentive to skimp on effort, since the payoff does not depend on the outcome. This occurs when an individual with insurance drives too carelessly, or when an artist with an agreed price for a commission passes too much work to underlings.

Fortunately, an environment of high trust tugged back on moral hazard. Nevertheless, some works still disappointed. When they did, patrons often took action. The examples already considered reveal a range of possible measures, from moving a portrait to a less prominent location to having it adapted or destroyed. The threat of a punishing patronal action helped to incentivize quality. Threats carried out raised the credibility of future threats. The potential for patrons to react negatively helped to promote the quality and appropriateness of commissions, thus dampening reception risks.

Patrons had a broad portfolio of actions to express their dissatisfaction because of a perceived lack of skill, beauty, or quality. Those actions fall into a half dozen categories (Figure 24).

All caused artists to suffer. They lost time, compensation, or reputation, and often all three. Patrons almost always lost out as well, when compared to a satisfactory completion. A price reduction, for example, did not fully compensate for a work that disappointed or displeased. Taken together, these six categories of patron action provide a taxonomy for considering the negative responses to art. Many of these actions also apply to non-commissioned paintings and sculptures, such as replacing a work or not obtaining an additional one from an artist who disappointed.

Potential Actions by Dissatisfied Patrons	
1	reduced compensation
2	work relocated
3	commission truncated or artist not rehired
4	major revisions required
5	work rejected
6	work destroyed

Figure 24 Potential Actions by Dissatisfied Patrons

First, patrons and their representatives often tried to pay painters and sculptors less than originally agreed. A disappointed patron or buyer might seek to reduce compensation for substandard work. An artist who felt cheated, as discussed in Section 2, might react by refusing to sell his work. Very often, at least in Italy, financial compensation and disputes were settled by an evaluating committee (O'Malley, 2005: 120–9), such as the one that assessed Ghirlandaio's altarpiece for Elisabetta Aldobrandini. Vasari tells us that after a committee examined Giovanni Rustici's sculpture depicting the Baptism of St John, for the Florentine Baptistry, it valued the work at 1200 florins instead of the 2000 originally agreed (Vasari, 1912–15, 8: 115; for payments, Mozzati, 2008: 79 n. 380). Financial penalties could be combined with other punitive actions. After Leonardo Buonafè received the *Madonna and Child with Saints* (Florence) (Figure 25) he had commissioned from Rosso Fiorentino, he refused to pay the full amount. Beyond reducing its price, Buonafè placed the altarpiece not in the major Florentine church of Ognissanti, as originally planned, but in a small countryside church of Santo Stefano. This change of locale also required the transformation of one saint depicted in the work from Leonard in honor of the patron, to Stephen (Ekserdjian, 2021: 40; Nova, 2021: 7–8).

Thus, a second possible action is to place a disappointing work in a less prestigious location than originally planned. This was the measure King Louis XIV took with Bernini's equestrian monument. A downgraded location hits the artist's reputation. For example, King Philip II of Spain commissioned El Greco's *Martyrdom of Saint Maurice* (Figure 26) to decorate the altar in the basilica of El Escorial (González García, 2018). One contemporary account states that the king found it unsatisfactory. Though El Greco was still generously compensated, his altarpiece was relegated to the sacristy (Arroyo Esteban, 2013). If the original location lacked decoration, as in this example, the patron would often need to pay for a replacement. El Greco's reputation in Spain took still another blow in 1584 when Romulo Cincinnato's altarpiece on

Figure 25 Rosso Fiorentino, *Enthroned Madonna and Child with Four Saints,* 1518, oil on panel, Gallerie degli Uffizi, Florence. Photo: Alinari Archives / George Tatge / Art Resource, NY.

the same subject, the *Martyrdom of Saint Maurice,* received pride of place in the basilica.

Third, displeased patrons regularly abrogated agreements with artists for future work. In his life of Sodoma, Vasari (1912–15, 7: 256) recounted that the artist produced two altarpieces for the Pisa Cathedral, a *Lamentation* and a *Sacrifice of Isaac,* but the dissatisfied patron "who had intended to have him paint some altarpieces for the church, dismissed him." Payment records help confirm the story: Sodoma received an advance in 1540 for a third altarpiece, but never completed the work. Moreover, these advance funds were counted as part of his compensation for the *Lamentation* (Ciardi, 1995: 138). In the same church, Giovann'Antonio Sogliani was commissioned to paint three altarpieces, but one came out poorly. Hence, the commission was transferred to Vasari, who completed the remaining two panels (Vasari, 1912–15, 7: 256).

Sometimes, contracts included a safety measure: works would be evaluated in progress. For the Parma Cathedral, Alessandro Araldi received a commission

Figure 26 El Greco, *Martyrdom of Saint Maurice*, 1580–81, oil on canvas, Monasterio de San Lorenzo, El Escorial. Photo: Wikimedia.

to paint the vaults west of the cupola but was told that he would be allowed to continue only if his work pleased the Board of Works (Smyth, 1997: 9–11). Similarly, and in the same city, Bernardino Gatti's contract for frescoes in the dome in the Church of the Steccata stipulated that the commissioners would sit in judgment on his work once it reached a certain stage. Then they would decide whether he should be allowed to continue.

Fourth, patrons, or other figures of authority, could demand that a finished work be revised, as did Louis XIV with the equestrian monument. Paolo Veronese's *Last Supper*, made in 1573 for the Dominican convent of San Giovanni and Paolo in Venice provides another famous example. The Tribunal of the Holy Inquisition ordered that the artist justify the presence of several details, including "buffoons,

Figure 27 Paolo Veronese, *Feast in the House of Levi,* 1573, oil on canvas, Galleria dell'Accademia, Venice. Photo: Wikimedia.

drunkards, Germans, dwarfs, and similar scurrilities" (Kaplan, 1997: 110). After the hearing, Veronese removed a few figures and changed the title of the work to *Feast in the House of Levi* (Figure 27). In yet another celebrated case, the Florentine Cathedral Board of Works, in 1436, determined that Paolo Uccello's *John Hawkwood* should be destroyed because it was "not painted as was deemed fitting." In the end, the artist repainted significant sections of the fresco; the painting survived. First, however, Uccello revised the original composition drawing which, according to his contract, he had to submit in 1433 (Melli, 1999). The requirement for the drawing, a measure intended to prevent an unsatisfactory painting, worked weakly. The extant sheet reveals that some sections from the first version were re-employed while others were modified, surely in response to the harsh criticism.

Fifth, patrons could outright reject a commissioned work, as did Averardo Salviati with Fra Bartolomeo's *Madonna*, mentioned in Section 1. But such rejections were rare. The use of preparatory drawing and models, together with discussions between artists and advisors, usually allowed patrons to nip the most egregious reception risks in the bud. One exception was Federico Zuccari's *Miraculous Procession of Saint Gregory*, commissioned in 1580 by Pope Gregory XIII for his family chapel in the church of Santa Maria del Barracano in his native Bologna (Ekserdjian, 2021: 41). The completed altarpiece, now lost, evidently appealed to some viewers given that it was reproduced in an engraving by Aliprando Caprioli dated 1581. However, that same year, the Pope not only rejected the work but refused to pay Zuccari. Gregory recommissioned the altarpiece from Cesare Aretusi, and his version, still in Bologna, differs from Zuccari's. Documents do not specify why the Pope objected to Zuccari's original altarpiece, but the nude plague victims so prominent in the foreground of the related engraving are not to be found in Aretusi's replacement.

Our sixth category is the most dramatic. The patron could destroy a commissioned work, a fate that *John Hawkwood* narrowly escaped. In the 1580s, King Philip II of Spain invited the Italian painter Federico Zuccari to create two altarpieces at El Escorial, as well as a fresco cycle in the cloister. Unfortunately, none of these works met with the king's favor. Though Zuccari was well paid, his altarpieces were repainted or replaced. His frescoes were destroyed, then substituted with another cycle by Pellegrino Tibaldi (Di Giampaolo, 1993; González García, 2018). In his life of Dosso and Battista Dossi, Vasari (1912–15, 5: 140) recounts that when their frescoes at the Villa Imperiale in Pesaro were unveiled, the works "proved to be so ridiculous that they left the service of the Duke Francesco Maria della Rovere in disgrace. He was forced to throw to the ground all that they had executed, and to have the frescoes repainted by others after the designs of Genga." Vasari's colorful account surely exaggerated. Some of Dossi's frescoes still adorn the villa.

As noted in Section 1, political upheavals often lead to the destruction of works. In 1355, for example, Doge Marino Faliero launched a coup against Venice's ruling aristocrats. The coup failed and he was beheaded. Then insult followed injury. A year later the Venetian government ordered that his portrait in the town hall be painted over and replaced with a damning inscription (Tobey, 2013: 22).

Religious upheavals led to destruction on a broader scale. In Florence at the end of the fifteenth century, an unimaginable turn of events put a large quantity of art and other luxury goods at risk. Fra Girolamo Savonarola famously organized two bonfires of the vanities. His followers confiscated and destroyed works of art thought to be offensive, including paintings of nudes by Botticelli. Neither the artists nor patrons could have anticipated this hazard, and thus it merits the label of ignorance. Surely, the most consequential example of an event beyond anticipation that led to the destruction of art occurred a few decades later in Northern Europe. A German friar, Martin Luther, posted his objections to the Catholic Church. Iconoclasm, and its sweeping consequences, followed. The next section starts with a discussion of that Iconoclasm, then turns to risks in the marketplace.

4 Risky Business: Northern Images After the Reformation, by Larry Silver

Across Europe, risks were a persistent ingredient of art transactions, whether those transactions involved commissions or third-party sales. Whatever the locale, whatever the product, production and reception risks imposed major losses. In the North, as this section details, Van Goyen and Vermeer were victims of the former; Rubens and Rembrandt suffered from the latter. Indeed, these losses, and a cascade of others, led all but the wealthy Rubens to die in poverty.

Some of these risks resulted from participants' actions. But others involved seismic developments in the societies where they resided. Perhaps no European period was so fraught with shifting concepts of religion and politics as the long sixteenth century, which witnessed the splitting of a united Church as well as the rise of newly consolidated nation-states that were increasingly centralized and dynastic (Greengrass, 2014). Across the continent, various Protestant sects disputed whether any religious images were permissible, given the dangers of idolatry. The very production of religious art became risky at best. Indeed, outbreaks of religious image-breaking, or iconoclasm, erupted frequently across the century – first in Luther's German-speaking regions during the 1520s, and most notably under Calvinist ideology in the Netherlands, starting in 1566 (Hofmann, 1983). Although Germany's 1555 Peace of Augsburg ultimately compromised on a doctrine that the regional ruler had the right to name his region's religion (*cuius regio, eius religio*), artists still risked offending their ruler. Thus, the profound political and religious shifts across Northern Europe placed new constraints on all public art, especially in those regions undergoing rapid change. One such place was the German city of Nuremberg.

Nuremberg Art (1520s)

Luther's creed spread rapidly across Germany during the 1520s, particularly in cities. The independent, imperial city of Nuremberg, chafing under its local bishop of Bamberg, formally adopted the new faith through its city council in 1525 (Strauss, 1976: 154–86). Local monasteries were dissolved, and the very existence of religious art was opened to debate. While Luther still permitted religious images for spiritual instruction, around Nuremberg some image destruction occurred (Christensen, 1979: 42–65). Fortunately, celebrated local works, such as the great pendant carved and painted limewood *Annunciation of the Rosary* (1517–18) by Nuremberg sculptor Veit Stoss (act. 1477–1533) in the church of St. Lorenz was covered up, preserved on orders by the city council due to respect for its local patrician patron, Anton II Tucher (Kahsnitz, 1983: 194–209).

In the wake of Nuremberg's adoption of Lutheranism, its most famous artist, Albrecht Dürer (1471–1528) began to paint a pair of large panels, often called the *Four Apostles* (though Saint Paul was not an apostle) (1526; Munich; Figure 28) (Christensen, 1979: 181–206; Goldberg, Heimberg, and Schawe, 1998: 478–559, no. 14). But rather than supplying them to a church setting, the artist gifted them instead to Nuremberg's city council. In this work, over-life-sized figures of these four holy men stand above calligraphic biblical quotes in Luther's German

Figure 28 Albrecht Dürer, *Four Apostles,* 1526, oil on panel, Alte Pinakothek, Munich. Photo: Wikimedia.

translation from their respective Gospels. Their texts underscore the Reformer's theological doctrine, to emphasize only the pure Gospel text, *sola scriptura*. By featuring Paul and John as the foremost figures, Dürer signals Luther's own Gospel preferences: "John's Gospel is the one, fine, true, and chief gospel, and is far to be preferred to the other three." For Luther, the epistles of Saint Paul and Saint Peter far surpass the Gospels of Mark, Matthew, and Luke (Price, 2003: 258). Significantly, the painting shows Peter's letter about false prophets (2 Peter 2: 1–3): "there will be false teachers among you, who will secretly bring in destructive heresies, even denying the Lord." Instead of depicting Peter as the first pope, as was traditional in Catholic art, Dürer gave him a new role.

The chosen Gospel passages, inscribed beneath the figures, follow warning words in German by Dürer himself:

> Let all worldly rulers in these perilous times take proper precaution lest they follow human inducement instead of the Word of God. For God wants nothing added to His Word nor yet taken away from it. Therefore, hear these four excellent men, Peter, John, Paul, and Mark, and heed their warning (Ashcroft, 2017: 819, 816).

Thus, the artist used his painting for a cautionary address to that same city council which had just sanctioned Nuremberg's turn to Lutheranism, and he also accompanied this pictorial donation with a personal letter to the council.

In his personal assessment of Nuremberg's current religious tensions, Dürer consciously took grave risk. He presented an austere work of art during an era when all religious art itself was being challenged and was shaken further socially by the previous year's Peasants' War, a revolt which Luther condemned (Roper, 2017: 259–72). Moreover, already in early 1525, a talented trio of younger Nuremberg artists close to Dürer was briefly expelled from the city and called "godless painters" (Müller and Schauerte, 2011). Thus, Dürer's *Four Apostles* risked its own controversy, even as it couched its explicit (Gospel-based) declarations about true faith in cautious general terms. Dürer also recast the task of religious art-making and moved it away from traditional devotional image representations of Jesus. Yet, in the process, the artist successfully secured a personal legacy in his own hometown.

Nuremberg's new religious controversies also affected other media, especially traditional carved religious altarpieces. The last major work (Figure 29) by the aged Veit Stoss, a large carved altarpiece devoted to the Virgin Mary, ran afoul of changing circumstances just as it neared completion. Commissioned in 1520 by his son Andreas, prior of the Carmelite convent

Figure 29 Veit Stoss, *Bamberg altarpiece*, 1523, wood, Bamberg Cathedral, Bamberg. Photo: Wikimedia.

of Nuremberg, and approved on the basis of a presentation drawing (now in Cracow), the piece became redundant when the city council closed all monasteries in 1525. Fortunately, the work was returned to the artist and later found a home as the high altar of Andreas's own Carmelite Church of the Assumption in Catholic Bamberg (Kahsnitz, 1983: 33–50; Kahsnitz, 2006: 402–19). Unlike his local *Annunciation with the Rosary*, recently completed, Stoss deliberately left this large, hinged fir ensemble unpainted, a recent development in German sculpture. He also personally carved it without any workshop assistance. The local sculptor surely hoped that, like Dürer's *Four Apostles*, his altarpiece would also serve as a virtuoso personal memorial in his hometown. Once rejected from its original destination, however, it was reduced from the ambitious original drawing layout. The final work still presented some narrative scenes on its wings, now carved in shallow relief, but its predella below was eliminated, and its elaborate narrative crown with ornament omitted. As further insult, Stoss's later appeal for final payment was also refused. In short, when Stoss died by 1533, his lifelong vocation as a carver of religious altarpieces had abruptly ended because of the contested image debates within Reformation Nuremberg.

Indeed, the entire great tradition of carved German altarpieces died a sudden death with the Reformation. Michael Baxandall quotes an appeal from around 1525 by painters and sculptors of Strasbourg, reporting the artists'

> pressing need ... since veneration of images has, through the word of God, now sharply fallen away and every day falls still more ... [and] we have learned to do nothing else but paint, carve, and the like ... (Baxandall, 1980: 69–82)

Carving had to continue in other forms, including work in luxury materials, such as marble or bronze, and often on a collectable personal scale, frequently featuring either mythological subjects or portraits (Smith, 1985).

Netherlands (1560s and after)

Even more than Lutheranism, Calvinism strictly forbade the display of religious images in churches (Finney, 1999; Mochizuki, 2008). While Calvinism's inroads into Netherlandish worship intensified during the 1560s, the doctrine already affected religious artists' careers during the 1550s. Especially in Antwerp's leading art center, two contemporaries, Pieter Aertsen (1507/08–1575) and Pieter Bruegel (act. 1551–69) strategized their painted outputs to avoid risk.

Pieter Aertsen continued to paint traditional, folding-wing religious altarpieces for churches. Surviving drawings confirm how carefully he prepared his images from preliminary ink drawings, often using intermediate full-scale cartoons for his

Figure 30 Pieter Aertsen, *Nebuchadnezzar*, ca. 1570, oil on panel, Museum
Boijmans Van Beuningen, Rotterdam. Photo: Wikimedia.

final compositions. But the 1566 regional destructions of religious art in churches
hit his work hard. Aertsen's biographer in 1604, Karel van Mander, describes the
artist's disconsolate reaction to such losses:

> Pieter was often [in an] incensed state of mind, because his artworks, which
> he hoped to leave behind as a memorial to his person, were destroyed. He
> directed himself toward the vandals of art in often strong terms and thus
> brought himself into danger. [author translation]

To reduce personal risk, some artists responded to contemporary religious
politics indirectly through biblical narrative. Aertsen himself, then working in
safety in Amsterdam, used the narrative of Nebuchadnezzar to attack Spanish
tyranny in his large-scale painting (ca. 1570; Rotterdam; Figure 30) (Kloek and
Halsema-Kubes, 1986: 408–10). The story (Daniel 3) exemplifies righteous,
monotheistic conduct by three youths who resist the tyrant's command to
worship his monumental gold cult statue with the rest of the populace.

Thrown into a fiery furnace, the three were protected from flames by an angel. That miracle led the king, in turn, to proclaim the signs and wonder of the Lord. Aertsen's vertical painting shows a host of tiny figures, dwarfed by the colossal statue in ancient armor, with the small furnace obscurely placed at the top left horizon. An attentive viewer must seek out the dim figures of the three youths and their angelic protector within its yellow-orange flames, far beyond the picture's main focus, which remains the king's giant effigy.

The Fiery Furnace as a biblical epitome about idolatry had already appeared in the famous Zurich Disputation on images from 1523, invoked by radical Swiss reformer Ulrich Zwingli to contrast true Christians with false idolators. John Calvin also used this subject to attack church images as no better than idols:

> Whoever bestows any kind of veneration on an Idol . . . acknowledges it to be God, and he who gives the name divinity to an Idol withholds it from God. Accordingly, the three companions of Daniel have taught us what estimate to form of this dissimulation . . . [L]et us learn by their example that to perform any acts of idolatry, in order to gain the favor of man, is more to be shunned than death in its most fearful form.
>
> On Shunning the Unlawful Rites of the Ungodly and Preserving the Purity of the Christian Religion (1537, as quoted by Moxey, 1977: 245–46; Eire, 1986: 197–233)

Consequently, iconoclastic hostility against religious images remained a live issue in the Netherlands well after 1566, still tied to interlocking contests between political leadership and its associated religion.

The younger artist, Pieter Bruegel, began his career as a prolific draftsman, including numerous designs for prints, made by professional engravers for publishing in Antwerp by *Aux Quatre Vents*, the printing firm of Hieronymus Cock (act. 1550–70) (Orenstein, 2001; Van Grieken, Luijten, and Van der Stock, 2013). Although documented in 1551 – the same year he entered the Antwerp painters' guild – as a young collaborator on the exterior of a lost altarpiece for the glovers' guild in Mechelen, Pieter Bruegel never again worked on any religious altarpiece in the increasingly charged religious atmosphere of the Netherlands (Marnef, 1996). Eventually, with the restoration of Catholicism in Antwerp, other artists, led by Maarten de Vos, would refill cathedral chapels with replacement altarpieces for the ones lost after the 1566 iconoclastic losses (Fabri and Van Hout, 2009; Freedberg, 2012; Jonckheere, 2012).

Bruegel did paint individual religious images as single panels, but (as far as we know), they wound up in private collections, probably as individual commissions. Their forms and content also differ from conventional altarpiece imagery. Bruegel turned to seemingly inoffensive subjects, such as the parables of Jesus (*Parable of the Sower*, 1557; *Blind Leading the Blind*, 1568), even though such contrasts between righteous followers and the deaf or blind held the potential to assert veiled opinions about correct religious views. Some Bruegel pictures represent rare Old Testament subjects. Some feature tyrants (*Tower of Babel*, 1563; *Suicide of Saul*, 1562), seemingly as an early, if veiled, criticism of Spanish-imposed Catholic religious authority in the region (Jonckheere, 2014; Silver, 2014). Karel van Mander's 1604 biography of Bruegel in his *Schilder-Boeck* also reports that the artist destroyed some of his own harsher work during a terminal illness to avoid the risk of political reprisals on his widow and sons. This danger, rarely documented for early modern art, remains familiar today in the form of censorship or suppression of visual imagery, and it provides an example of the potential pressure on an artist to self-censor to trim personal risk.

Bruegel's *Massacre of the Innocents* (ca. 1566; Hampton Court; several copies) transposes a biblical scene of mayhem (Matthew 2: 16–18) into a wintry Flemish village with contemporary armor and weapons (pikes and halberds) (Fishman, 1982; Kunzle, 2002: 219–35). The horrors inflicted here by red-coated soldiers, silhouetted against snowy background, can thus be read as having contemporary resonance. They cruelly slaughter children and terrorize their mothers, who resist in vain while troops break into their houses. So terrible were those images of dead children on the ground or in their mothers' laps that a later owner of the painting had them painted out and replaced with slaughtered barnyard animals and bundles (Campbell, 1985: 13–20). Thus, at personal risk, even for a private client, Bruegel stages a biblical scene as both contemporary and local to suggest covert criticism of current draconian measures imposed on the region by ruling Spanish overlords, identified with the image of biblical King Herod. In similar fashion, unrelenting pessimism in Bruegel's *Triumph of Death* (Madrid), likely from around the same late date, also includes contemporary armored soldiers among the universal victims of skeletal armies (Silver, 2015).

Controversies about religious art in the Netherlands climaxed in a Calvinist-inspired destruction of church images in August 1566 (Freedberg, 1988; Arnade, 2008: 125–65). Simultaneously, in the nascent Dutch Revolt, regional political authority oscillated between local political resistance and reasserted Spanish control. After 1567, one particularly harsh backlash by the Duke of Alba resulted in punishments known as the Council of Troubles (Arnade, 2008: 166–211; Darby, 2001). Thus, artistic risk periodically could attend any attempt to celebrate political authority through the image of a ruler, lest shifts in the fortune of war undermine current favorable conditions.

Significantly, in May 1571, Alba commissioned a commanding bronze statue of himself for the Antwerp citadel (Figure 31) from leading local sculptor Jacques Jongelinck (Becker, 1971; Arnade, 2008, 199–209). Based on the

Figure 31 Jacques Jongelinck (engraving after statue by), *Statue of the Duke of Alba*, from Pieter Bor, *Nederlantsche Oorloghen*, ca. 1621, engraving. Peace Palace Library. Photo: Wikimedia.

model of a celebratory full-length bronze of *Emperor Charles V Restraining Fury* by Leone Leoni (1549–55; Madrid), it showed Alba in armor, conquering a supine, two-headed, six-armed personified creature, Rebellion and Heresy. These two destroyed nemeses – from a Spanish viewpoint – had vainly resisted Alba's authority in both politics and religion. More pointedly, the bronze for the

Figure 32 Hendrick Goltzius, *William the Silent,* c. 1581, engraving,
Rijksmuseum, Amsterdam. Photo: Rijksmuseum, Amsterdam.

statue came from cannons Alba captured from rebels in battle. His statue
gestures with an extended right hand, palm downward, as if offering clemency,
while also showing command with the left hand through a military baton. Alba's
statue enjoyed only short-lived prominence in Antwerp because the duke came
to personify both the hubris and cruelty of Spanish rule. Indeed, in 1573,
William of Orange, leader of the Dutch Revolt, compared the duke to the
biblical Babylonian tyrant Nebuchadnezzar (Daniel 3). In June 1574, the Alba
statue was removed and melted down for more armaments.

In 1581, Dutch engraver Hendrick Goltzius (1558–1617) made a political portrait of Alba's antagonist, *William the Silent* (Figure 32), head of the House of
Orange and leader of the Dutch Revolt. In his public print, Goltzius took the short-
term risk of such political glorification (Leeflang and Luijten, 2004: 67–9). Prince
William, armored in half-length, carries the baton of command, like Alba's statue,

with his coat of arms above. Goltzius's preliminary drawing layout (Amsterdam) framed the portrait with allegories that extol his virtues: Pure Religion, Faithful Sentinel, Careful Government. In the final print, however, four marginal rectangles assert the religious nature of the Revolt and identify William with Moses, protected by divine providence while combining true religion with political leadership. At the lower right, an emblem bears the prince's motto: "calm amidst raging seas." It shows the divine hand wielding a sword beneath a cloud against driving winds, while a bird's nest floats atop whitecap waves. The Latin cartouche beneath the portrait defines William's risky confrontation in the current conflict that he leads: "The violent godless must tremble. This one care occupies me, Lord Christ, that so long as I live, undaunted by the arduous dangers, I can protect Thy law, the flock entrusted to me, and the sacred privileges of the fatherland." During the 1580s, Goltzius also produced numerous individual portrait engravings of other Revolt activists: military leaders, known rebels, and sympathetic foreign leaders. Fortunately, his Haarlem-based audience would approve, but had the fortunes of war shifted, his very life would have been endangered.

Political Rejection – Rubens and Rembrandt

Even the most successful artists risked rejection, especially if they crossed their patrons or misread the political situation around their contract commissions. Peter Paul Rubens (1577–1640), one of the best connected, wealthiest artists of the seventeenth century and a man knighted by three different kings, still encountered political difficulties at the highest level in his role as a painter-diplomat. Within his successful, enormous cycle of twenty-four canvases (1622–24) made for the Queen Mother of France, Marie de' Medici, Rubens had to repaint one painting to smooth over internal political conflict with her own son, King Louis XIII (Held, 1980: 87–128; Millen and Wolf, 1989; Renger and Denk, 2002: 393–443).

That planned historical scene was rejected for its candor, deemed unworthy of the queen's dignity: her embarrassing *Flight from Paris* (1622; Munich). In May 1617, Marie was forced by her son and heir to flee from Paris to the chateau of Blois. Rubens shows her leaving the city gate to a carriage with her ladies-in-waiting, ousted by personified evil, Calumnia, with a torch and two flying harpies. Marie's true antagonist was the newly emergent Cardinal Richelieu, minister of war and favorite of her son, the newly empowered young King Louis XIII. That image of humiliation was replaced by a sunny allegorical eulogy: *Felicity of the Regency* (Silver, 2008).

The Queen also planned a complementary sequel by the artist to honor her late husband, King Henri IV (d. 1610). That cycle was eliminated entirely, even

Figure 33 Peter Paul Rubens, *Triumphal Entry of Henri IV into Paris,* 1627–1630, oil on canvas, Gallerie degli Uffizi, Florence. Photo: Wikimedia.

after several preparatory sketches and several canvases already in an advanced state of completion (Jost, 1964; du Bourg, 2017). One of the most finished pictures, with Rubens's distinctive *bravura* brushwork, *The Triumphal Entry of Henri IV into Paris* (ca. 1628–31; Figure 33), is staged like an ancient Roman civic ritual. Rubens also sketched battle scenes and other major life events, such as Henri's birth, his courtship of Marie de' Medici, and his coronation. Six large sketches remained in Rubens's estate.

Rubens was delighted by the opportunity to paint in the grand manner for Luxembourg Palace's other walls, especially for masculine scenes of military conquest and royal heroism. But he was undermined by the passive-aggressive royal favorite, Cardinal Richelieu, who prevailed on the Queen Mother to choose an Italian artist instead. Eventually, the entire project was dropped. After the Queen Mother finally went into exile in 1631, all prospects for the *Henri IV* series effectively ended, the victim of conflicting politics in France during the Thirty Years War. This was the basis of the political tension surrounding the painting project. Whereas Rubens had pursued peace on behalf of his Spanish regents in Brussels, Richelieu supported France's entry into the conflict, and Richelieu ultimately prevailed, scuttling Rubens's opportunity.

Rembrandt (1606–69) also lost a major contribution due to political – and possibly aesthetic – controversy. To decorate the gallery of the huge new Amsterdam Town Hall (dedicated 1655), a distinguished group of artists, including Rembrandt, was commissioned to paint episodes from the legendary

Figure 34 Rembrandt van Rijn, *The Oath of Claudius Civilis*, 1661–2, oil on
canvas, Nationalmuseum, Stockholm. Photo: Wikimedia.

ancient revolt against the Roman Empire by local tribal natives, the Batavians
(Van de Waal, 1974: 28–43; Carroll, 1986). That rebellion was read as the
prefiguration of the newly successful Dutch Revolt against the mighty empire of
Spain.

Rembrandt's subject was the nighttime conspiratorial *Oath of Claudius
Civilis* (Figure 34). His huge canvas shows life-sized figures in half-length at
a ritual meal, taking their solemn oath of rebellion over conjoined swords.
However, for unknown reasons, Rembrandt's work was rejected and replaced
with a substitute.

Displeasure about the painting likely stemmed from the artist's unflatteringly
frank, frontal depiction of the crowned Batavian leader, which showed his missing
eye as well as his unheroic, rough-hewn companions. Moreover, Rembrandt's bold,
sketchy brushwork and acidic coloration might have disappointed his patrons
during a period when Dutch art increasingly prized finer, finished surfaces.
Despite being allocated his prominent space, Rembrandt had nevertheless violated
the emphasis on heroism and decorum that prevailed in Dutch history painting and
elsewhere in the Town Hall's commissioned pictures. His bold pictorial risk cost
him the opportunity to contribute to Amsterdam's newest, grandest, most public art.
Like Veit Stoss's altarpiece, Rembrandt's work survived, but cut down considerably, so any intended personal legacy to his hometown wound up rejected, reduced,
and relocated – the epitome of *reception risk*.

Antwerp's Art Market Risks

Risky economic outcomes also permeated art making in an emerging open market. The sixteenth-century financial metropolis of Antwerp established the first open art market, first located at the major city square near the church of Our Lady, but soon relocated to its own nearby site, the *Pand* (Ewing, 1990; Vermeylen, 2003; Silver, 2006). In marketing artworks to a general public, successful pictorial types, such as frolicking peasants in taverns, or landscapes (with or without saintly figures) became favorite images repeatedly produced by increasingly specialized art-makers. For example, Joachim Patinir (act. 1515–24), was already described by the visiting Albrecht Dürer in his diary as "the good landscape painter" (Vergara, 2007; Ashcroft, 2017: 579). Such close association between an artist — whether a designer of prints or a painter – and his favorite subject-matter led to the formation of recognizable pictorial brands, such as Patinir's landscapes. Similarly, Hieronymus Bosch's Hell scenes with inventive monsters were often copied, imitated, or faked by later artists, testament to his lasting popularity across the sixteenth century (Unverfehrt, 1980; Silver, 2006: 133–60).

Within that market setting, pictorial innovation rapidly crystallized into fixed types, as successful formulas cultivated predictable conventions for their avid consumers. Even originally mixed subjects, such as landscapes with saints, resulted in replicable images of favorite subjects, made familiar and reinforced through repeated sales to an increasingly wider public. A print market began to codify favorite imagery in affordable formats. Bruegel's print designs for his Antwerp publisher Hieronymus Cock included formulaic landscapes, peasant scenes, and even Boschian monsters, and the far cheaper, multiple images of prints further accelerated this marketing process.

Artists increasingly identified their work by adding their signatures, largely absent from the works of major fifteenth-century painters in the Netherlands (though early engravings often bore initials because of their close association with trademarks of metalworkers, whose skills gave rise to engraving on metal matrixes for printing). Signatures offered little protection, given fakes and forgeries. Indeed, one of Bruegel's earliest print designs for Cock, *Big Fish Eat Little Fish* (1557), was actually credited to "Hieronymus Bos inventor" in order to ensure readier sales for the work by associating it with Bosch, the deceased popular artist, instead of an unfamiliar newcomer (Bassens and Van Grieken, 2019: 26–27). Later artists, in turn, imitated Bruegel's successful peasant subjects and his landscape formulas; in some cases, mostly drawings, they occasionally forged his signature.

As artists repeated their formulas, they increasingly became specialists in pictorial types. Patinir occasionally collaborated with fellow specialists to combine his landscape settings with their large-figure compositions (Silver, 2006: 161–85). In the specialist world of print production after midcentury, designers like Bruegel also collaborated with a production team – almost like a Hollywood movie studio (Silver, 2013) – comprised of other specialists, such as professional engravers and print publishing staffs.

With such strategies of repeatable genres, brand-name associations with known artists and their popular formulas, and – in the case of prints – new, efficient collaborative publishing production procedures, risks in the open market were considerably reduced. As a result, previous sales successes soon converted hard-to-assess uncertainties into more modest, reliable risks.

What was once a market innovation involving risk could soon became an established pictorial genre on the open art market. A good example is the bold new large-scale peasant imagery by both Aertsen and Bruegel, which became a major subject for later Netherlandish artists, extending well into the seventeenth century. Its initial innovative force as a novelty subject for large-scale painting succeeded in the art marketplace and thus quickly became a staple for increasingly specialized painters, whose individual differences established their personal brand (Raupp, 1986: 195–304; Silver, 2006: 103–23; Van der Coelen and Lammertse, 2015: 177–97). Prior images of peasants had primarily preoccupied only German printmakers, including Dürer, but first Aertsen and then Bruegel innovated with new, large-scale peasant subjects as paintings. Scholars have noted the visual paradox of elevating such humble figures into monumental scale, usually reserved for heroic subjects (Falkenburg, 1989; Falkenburg, 1995). From peasant subjects, in turn, other novel imagery emerged, including kitchen and market scenes, which would generate increasing attention to commodity still-life. Aertsen with his nephew Joachim Beuckelaer became principal first practitioners of both kitchen and market scenes (Honig, 1998: 1–99; Silver, 2006: 87–132). Painted market scenes, as Elizabeth Honig has pointed out, could also epitomize the very art market consumer society in which such images were sold.

For most practitioners, the peasant largely offered an object of ridicule, particularly for his unrestrained excesses, especially gluttony (Silver, 2006, 103–23; Van der Coelen and Lammertse, 2015: 177–97). Bruegel's peasant imagery, exceptionally, often involves relatively more dignified peasant behavior, such as the *Peasant Wedding Feast* or even his *Kermis Dance* on a saint's name holiday (both ca. 1568; Vienna) (Gibson, 1991; Kavaler, 1999: 149–260). Additionally, he depicted productive peasant labor on the land, notably in the painted series, *The Seasons*, of which five survive (1565).

One Bruegel drawing of peasant labor, *The Beekeepers* (ca. 1568; Figure 35), makes a theme out of risk itself. It shows a foolhardy egg thief up a tree in contrast with careful apiculture. Here a coordinated group of peasants uses thick

Figure 35 Pieter Bruegel the Elder, Beekeepers, 1568, pen and brown ink, Staatliche Museen zu Berlin, Kupferstichkabinett. Photo: bpk Bildagentur / Jörg P. Anders / Art Resource, NY.

protective garments and wicker masks over their faces, rendering them collectively anonymous, while they act in concert, in harmony with nature, rather than boldly and singly like the nest-robber. An inscription on the drawing repeats a Flemish proverb regarding risk and reward: "He who knows the nest, knows it; he who robs it, has it" (Kavaler, 1999: 243–9). In effect, this drawing also serves as a metonym of Antwerp's early capitalism along with its attendant financial risks. It finds its painted analogue in Bruegel's famous *Fall of Icarus* (preserved in copies), which contrasts the tragically proud young hero's fall with the husbandry of plowman, angler, and shepherd as well as the sailing ship successfully headed into port like the great merchant ships that served the metropole (Baldwin, 1986; Kavaler, 1986; Silver, 1996).

Seventeenth-Century Holland Art Markets

Risks remained in the competitive open art market, and not all artists were successful (North, 1997; Rasterhoff, 2016). Many died poor or had to supplement their professional craft with additional sources of income, often as art dealers but sometimes from side occupations such as brewing. Sometimes they suffered from the intense competition from cheaper imported paintings from the South Netherlands (Israel, 1997; Sluijter, 2009). Other times, novel technical experiments were inefficient and/or presented visual difficulty for potential buyers. Two examples from Haarlem suggest the range of those harsh conditions, each a different example of *production risk.*

Despite being a major innovator in what is called Dutch "tonal landscape painting," Jan Van Goyen (1596–1656) died in poverty with massive debts, even after selling off his house and personal collection (Crenshaw, 2001: 17–27). Though greatly admired by contemporary observers, such as state secretary Constantijn Huygens in his commentaries on art (1629) or burgomaster Jan Orlers in his description of Leiden (1641), Van Goyen's prices remained quite low (Chong, 1987). In the wider world of capitalist risk, in 1636–7 Van Goyen also lost heavily in the famed Dutch investment bubble: tulips (Goldgar, 2007). He also worked as a picture dealer and appraiser, arranged auction sales, and made other speculative investments in land and houses.

As an artist, Van Goyen was a master of specialization. His restrained palette and formulaic diagonal repetition of favorite locations and motifs – dunes and rivers – enabled a prolific output of his mature work, especially during the 1640s. In technique, the artist's production was efficient; his limited color range reduced costs for pigments for his formulaic tonal landscapes, created rapidly with his distinctive thin brushstrokes (e.g. *View of Dordrecht from the North,* early 1650s; Figure 36). Economic historian John Michael Montias has

Figure 36 Jan van Goyen, *View of Dordrecht from the North,* early 1650s, oil on panel, National Gallery of Art, Washington D.C. Photo: National Gallery of Art, Washington D.C.

connected these adaptations both to process innovation as well as product innovation, where an artist establishes a recognizably personal, distinct pictorial brand in the market (Montias, 1987; Montias, 1990). Unfortunately, Van Goyen's numerous landscapes generated a vicious circle: because his works were priced inexpensively, he had to be prolific, generating over 1200 documented paintings and 800 drawings. His massive output kept his prices low. He never could achieve solvency. Van Goyen's student and son-in-law Jan Steen also suffered financial setbacks (Crenshaw, 2001).

Another contemporary Haarlem artist also lost in the intensely competitive Dutch art market and died young as well as poor. Hercules Segers (1589/90-after 1633) ceaselessly experimented, especially with etching and color printmaking techniques (Heuer, 2012; Leeflang and Roelofs, 2016). His surviving output is painfully small: 18 paintings and 54 etched plates, totaling 184 impressions. However, he might also have printed lost works, either cheap or ephemeral. Like Van Goyen, Segers chiefly created landscapes, but many of them (e.g., *The Enclosed Valley*, ca. 1625; Figure 37) look more like moonscapes, pitted mountain valleys with craggy rocks, utterly different from the increasingly popular local Dutch views rendered with familiar naturalism – a genre basic to Van Goyen and the other Haarlem tonal landscape painters. Segers was also fascinated with ruins and lone trees, made all the more evocative by his innovative colored inks, tinted papers, and innovative soft-ground and sugar-lift etching techniques. He also experimented with printing on

Figure 37 Hercules Segers, *The Enclosed Valley*, ca. 1625, line etching printed on linen, Rijksmuseum, Amsterdam. Photo: Rijksmuseum, Amsterdam.

linen, creatively mixing painting with printmaking. No two print impressions by Segers are alike; his professional difficulty clearly arose largely from his constant tinkering – in striking contrast to the assembly-line painted productions of Van Goyen.

Segers was remembered by a younger generation as a desperately unsuccessful genius. Rembrandt's pupil and art theorist Samuel van Hoogstraten, in his *Introduction to the High School of Painting* (1678), discusses Segers in a chapter, "How an Artist Has to Conduct Himself to Counter the Power of Fortune." He claims that "the unnoticed and yet artistically great Hercules Seghers" found no market for his works, even at minimal prices, so that his accomplished prints were even used as wrapping paper. As a result, forced to turn shirts and bedsheets into art works, in depression, he fell to his death downstairs while drunk (Van Hoogstraten, 2021: 215, 336). Legend perhaps, but still an artist's life ended in deep desperation due to failure in the art marketplace.

A similar outcome befell one of Holland's greatest painters, Johannes Vermeer (1632–75) (Montias, 1989). Meticulous in his oil paint technique, using slow-drying layers and expensive pigments to achieve persuasive effects of interior light, Vermeer produced fewer than fifty paintings, of which about forty survive. This represented a very meager output when compared to his peers, and a clear production risk. To survive, he had to charge high prices for his art. Quality and distinctiveness during a period of Holland's prosperity made this success viable at first. However, as the wider economy of Holland collapsed in 1672, following an invasion by King Louis XIV of France, financial pressures mounted on Vermeer and his large family, a wife and ten minor children. While he also practiced the sideline trade of art dealing, that income foundered as well during the economic recession, according to his widow. As a hedge against uncertain sales, Vermeer worked for one principal patron, Pieter Claesz van Ruijven (1624–74), perhaps on a first-refusal basis; but Ruijven died a year before the artist, another grave setback.

Other artists in seventeenth-century Holland also suffered financial setbacks, not least Rembrandt. After his initial meteoric rise in Amsterdam during the 1630s, Rembrandt made several bad investments and overextended himself with loans, for which he sometimes used artworks as security. His income woes eventually led to a 1656 bankruptcy (*cessio bonorum*) and the sale of his collection.

Earlier in his career, Rembrandt painted directly for dealers, who served as middlemen for his works. Later, however, his broadly brushed works disappointed some patrons, who insisted that he repaint or further finish their canvases (e.g., his *Juno*, c. 1662–65; Los Angeles, Hammer Museum) (Held, 1969: 85–103). Rembrandt's production style provoked several documented disputes with his clients (Crenshaw 2006: 110–35), compounded by his insistence on tacking on additional charges if he agreed to rework pictures to a patron's satisfaction. Working independently and stubbornly insisting on the high quality of his own work, he sometimes insisted on greater payment upon delivery, even from his one patron who was a ruler, the regent (stadtholder) Frederick Hendrick. On another occasion, he quarreled with a powerful local Amsterdam patrician, Andries de Graeff, over a delivered portrait. In another disagreement, about whether his work in progress was a poor likeness of a young woman, Rembrandt insisted on full payment before he would rework it; additionally, he threatened to put that decision up to a panel of art experts. Otherwise, he claimed, he would recall the work and put the portrait up for auction. One patron in distant Sicily tried to reduce the price on a commission, but the artist steadfastly resisted.

Rembrandt's out-of-fashion production risk, of seemingly "unfinished" style, also combined, as we saw already, with his political rejection from the Amsterdam Town Hall, to result in his most disappointing reception risk. Though modern studies of these famous artists seldom mention their hardships, in the seventeenth-century Dutch art market, a painting career clearly entailed many hazards. There was the risk of production – style as well as technique – and also the ultimate risk of reception, even of completed works, by their potential buyers.

In the early modern period, artists faced two major career dangers: market uncertainties, and criticisms on political and religious grounds.

5 Three Tales of Trust and Risk Reduction

The previous sections analyzed the array of risks in the art world. This concluding section analyzes how the taming of those risks enabled a thriving art business to develop in the premodern period. In the south of Europe, that business operated primarily through patronage for major works of art. In the north, an open market emerged in the early sixteenth century. By the next century, art markets had opened in nearly all major cities across Europe.

Patronage transactions tend to be *sui generis*. When a particular artist worked for an individual patron to produce a specified artwork, the risks depended on the particular commission. By contrast, in an open art market, the vast majority of art transactions involved similar products, such as landscape paintings, sold by many competing merchants and purchased by many customers. Mere inspection could reduce most risks in such markets. By analogy, think of customers squeezing melons to determine which ones to buy.

Ceccarelli (2021: 239) observed that the insurance market in the late Medieval and Renaissance periods functioned thanks in part to "the existence of a system of sanctions and rewards which, in their turn, were usually related to the so-called 'strong' ties (especially family, ethnic, and religious)." As we saw in Section 3, Eckstein would surely add an item to this list: living and praying within a "neighborhood." Ceccarelli further noted that marine insurance "might have also operated on the basis of 'weak' ties, in which contract enforcement was promoted by a complex combination of collective reputation and legal norms." In an open market, the number of weak ties tends to be high and grows as the market continues to develop.

Increased transactions facilitated the development of bonds among artists, patrons, buyers, and dealers. Those bonds in turn created the social capital that tamed risk and promoted trust. These elements, in combination, enabled the commercial and social networks of the Renaissance to flourish. To highlight some of the key variables in the Renaissance art world, we explore trust and risk-reducing methods in three very different situations. First is a commission, where an artist in late fourteenth-century Italy prepared a product under contract with an individual patron. Second is the "thick" art market in early-sixteenth century Antwerp. Third is a dealer in early seventeenth-century Amsterdam who purchased valuable works to resell at a profit. In each tale, the risks are clear, and trust plays a starring role in constraining them. In the first two cases, trust held; in the third, trust was violated, and the dealer got burned. As always when risks are meaningful, matters could have easily ended up differently.

Economists describe a market as "thick" when there are large numbers of both sellers and buyers. An example is the modern market for restaurant meals. Product quality is easy to compare, and participants can choose among many potential trade partners. Ties among participants, though almost all weak, are abundant. These features significantly limit risks. A thin market has but one or a few potential buyers or sellers for a product, often an unusual or unique product. High-end art dealers operated in a "thin" market (and still do). They mostly sold distinctive pieces and engaged with a limited set of potential buyers. Their ties with buyers were often strong but few. In such an environment, certain risks persisted, such as misattributions. The patronage market was thinner still, usually with a single artist and a specific patron, and often a product that would be of limited value to others. Risks, such as reduced payment, delayed delivery, and substandard quality are relatively high in thin markets.

Patronage

Our first story addresses the two primary production risks: for artists, contested payment, and for patrons, delayed or failed delivery. The story's protagonist, Francesco Datini (1360–1423), is often known as the "merchant of Prato," a city about eighteen kilometers from Florence (Origo, 1957). The survival of over 150,000 letters and other records make this extremely wealthy merchant one of the best-documented non-patricians of his day. As a teenager, Datini moved to Avignon, where he set up a successful company, then moved back to Prato in the 1380s. Correspondence from this latter phase shows Datini to be a prime example of Baker's thesis (2021: 74), that starting in "the fourteenth century, a new type of sedentary merchant began gradually to replace the roaming operator of earlier centuries, a transition requiring an increased reliance on others … interpersonal trust became fundamental to the operation of the Renaissance economy." Certainly, trust was key in Datini's efforts to decorate his home in Prato (Dunlop, 2009: 15–42). In 1391, he turned to a Florentine painter Niccolò di Pietro Gerini, the business partner of Tommaso del Mazza. Datini had strong ties with del Mazza, who had already worked for the merchant. When del Mazza fell ill, Datini's trust in him spilled over to Gerini. This phenomenon illustrates reputational externalities, discussed in Section 2. In the eyes of Datini, del Mazza's good reputation did not merely spill over to Gerini; it then spilled further to two other Florentine painters recommended by Gerini. The first was Bartolomeo di Bertozzo, a little-known artist, and the second was Agnolo Gaddi, one of the most famous painters then active in Florence.

By late September 1391, the three artists had taken up residence at Datini's palace in Prato; three months later, before they returned to Florence for Christmas, they requested compensation for the first phase of their work. A memo by Datini reveals that he had lost faith in all three painters; with each, he had only weak ties. Datini believed that they overcharged him, so he refused to pay and asked his agent to obtain more information about standard prices. (If Datini had done this earlier, he could have saved everyone a lot of time and effort.) The artists stopped working on Palazzo Datini and took on other commissions. The project got delayed, which certainly constituted a negative turn of events for the patron. A risk-reducing mechanism employed by Bartolomeo di Bertozzo resolved this stand-off. He brought his claim for 50 florins to his trade association, the Florentine Painters' guild. The guild named an artist to appraise the frescoes in Prato. Datini's agent had recommended this appraiser, which gave the patron a major advantage. However, the appraiser gave the frescoes high praise, so in 1392 Datini was required to pay 55 florins. The presence of an outside expert or committee, backed by an institution, reduced the risk that the painter's quality work would receive inadequate compensation. Though Datini must have been frustrated by these findings, they presumably reduced his concerns about overpayment, and certainly allowed work to continue at his home.

An adjudication process accepted as fair by both producers and consumers brings benefits to all. It removes random or inappropriate elements – such as a bullying patron – from compensation. This system worked in 1392, though one might have expected instead that a powerful and influential merchant would triumph in a dispute against an obscure artist. Similarly, a century later, the heirs of Filippo Strozzi, the wealthiest man in Florence, brought court proceedings against Filippino Lippi. The painter had started a fresco cycle in the Strozzi Chapel in Santa Maria Novella but refused to continue, for reasons not documented (Nelson, 2022: 145; Figure 38). The guild subsequently ordered the patron to increase the artist's compensation and Filippino, now assured fair payment, completed the fresco cycle.

Of course, some adjudicating bodies sided with patrons. We saw this in Section 2, when Elizabetta Aldobrandini succeeded in paying less for her substandard altarpiece by the Ghirlandaio workshop. Even when there were

Figure 38 Filippino Lippi, *Strozzi Chapel* (Altar Wall) detail, 1495–7, fresco, Santa Maria Novella, Florence. Photo: Wikimedia.

no disputes, appraisals could serve as part of the production-and-sale process. Often, artists and patrons agreed from the start that an outside expert would establish the value of the finished painting or sculpture. Both producers and consumers had a strong incentive to establish fair prices. When there are significant variations in quality for contracted pieces, it is essential to have mechanisms that can adjust compensation when works are complete. Otherwise, outcomes would be less fair. That is, superior and inferior work would be paid the same, rejected commissions would increase, and production risks would proliferate for artists and patrons alike. Moreover, the potential for downward price adjustments tends to keep quality up and reception risks down. If you short-change the buyer, you suffer a financial penalty. On the other hand, if you regularly produce works considered to be superlative, as did Raphael and Guido Reni (also discussed in Section 2), then you could command higher prices.

A Market with Guilds

In his discussion of a new conception of the future, which developed at the turn of the sixteenth century, Baker argues that, "merchants relied on institutional mechanisms and modes of behavior to mitigate against the unknowability of the future, to guard against breaches of trust, and to maintain honesty and fairness in trade" (Baker, 2021: 76). By the fourteenth century, some of these mechanisms, such as adjudicating bodies, were already active. Our second case considers the role of institutions in reducing two closely related hazards: the production risk for an artist when clients or patrons cannot be located; and the reception risk to artists and buyers that completed works will be ignored or criticized.

Artists' guilds dramatically reduced the probability that artists and buyers would suffer losses from these two types of risk. These institutions' first contribution was to foster quality. Often, guilds for artists and artisans required aspiring members to produce a "masterpiece," that is, a work of quality deemed worthy of a "master." In Valencia, the city government authorized in 1607 the creation of a painters' guild with an entrance exam (Falomir, 2006: 152). When neither masterpieces nor exams were required for membership, as in Antwerp, the guild of painters still closely regulated the long training and apprenticeships that were required for membership (Vermeylen and Van der Stichelen, 2006: 191). Even Gerard David, a distinguished painter from Bruges, had to register with the Antwerp guild to sell paintings there near the end of his career in 1515.

These measures, which limited or delayed membership, served to restrict competition, and thereby boost the economic interests of guild members. Similarly, today's tough exams and lengthy apprenticeships for electricians in the US keep numbers low and earnings high. Restrictive measures also served to establish and maintain a high level of quality. If you went to the open market in Antwerp, as described in Section 4, all the Flemish paintings on sale were produced by well-trained guild members. That measure reassured buyers, particularly those with limited ability to judge quality.

Members of guilds had a strong interest in keeping up the quality of the other members. Through the mechanism of reputational externalities, buyers extrapolated the quality of one guild member from the evidence of (or tales about) the quality of another; in much the same way, the reputations of today's physicians, lawyers, or professors spill over to other members of their practice, firm, or university. Imagine that after a purchase of a painting by a guild member at the Antwerp art market, a couple received confirmation that the quality was high. The owners would enjoy the painting in their home, where it was praised by visitors they wanted to impress. That would lead the couple to be more likely to trust another member of the guild when they returned to the same market, and they would probably pass their positive beliefs on to others. This confidence, complemented by guild guidelines regarding the quality of pigments, discussed in Section 2, reassured buyers at the market that the paintings for sale were well made.

A well-documented controversy in Rome reveals other means of institutional oversight for quality control at the upper end of the market. New regulations, published by the Art Academy in 1609, required that paintings valued at more than three scudi, "could be undertaken by non-academicians only with the written permission of the head of the Academy." Moreover, the head of the Academy assumed the responsibility of checking the quality of the most prestigious products: "every work of art made for the Pope or the city government" (Cavazzini, 2008: 45). A protest led by Roman artists gently relaxed these regulations. Nevertheless, artist associations everywhere recognized the need to signal their members' high quality to potential clients, expressly to bolster and spread reputational externalities.

The assurance of having a well-made work, produced with the proper materials and techniques, dramatically reduces the potential of substandard skill as a reception risk. The danger for artists that comes most frequently to mind, at least to most readers today, is a work rejected or criticized because of its style. Late fifteenth-century Florence painter Neri di Bicci found a way to reduce reception risks. Though twenty-first-century art lovers and authors focus their attention on Neri's contemporaries, such as Filippo Lippi and Botticelli, and though Neri never appeared on Renaissance lists of major painters, his career was remarkably successful and lucrative. Neri's winning formula was to develop a recognizable style that secured approval, and then stick with it.

Figure 39 Neri di Bicci, *Virgin and Child on the Throne*, fifteenth century, tempera and gold leaf on panel, Museu Nacional d'Art de Catalunya, Barcelona. Photo: Wikimedia.

Thus, the painter offered a set number of pictorial solutions with only minor variations (Holmes, 2003; Figure 39). Patrons knew what they would get and knew that the product would not be criticized. This low-risk proposition appealed both to patrons of altarpieces and buyers who acquired his ready-made Madonna paintings. This enhanced the trust of purchasers and slashed the risk of inadequate demand. Neri prospered.

We might think of a second-tier Italian artist of reliably staid altarpieces and Madonnas as falling in a separate category than the innovative Northern Europe painters who specialized in a particular genre. In both cases, however, we find a "recognizable pictorial brand," to borrow the phrase Larry Silver uses in Section 4 to describe Patinir's landscapes and Bosch's hellish scenes. These pictorial genre works first appeared in Antwerp, where, in comparison to the world of patronage in Neri di Bicci's Florence, the direct ties between a buyer and seller were weak. However, since Antwerp was a thick market, the resulting network of weak ties bolstered trust. As is common for ties and trust, high density compensated for low intensity. Moreover, numerous transactions in similar works facilitated information flow. Nevertheless, buyers did face the risk of changing tastes. After dune scenes became less popular, painters had to find a new subject to depict, and both they and dealers had to unload their dune stock.

The immense popularity of certain artists led to forgeries in the market, an immense risk for buyers who do not purchase directly from producers. In about 1560, Felipe de Guevara, a nobleman in the court of King Philip II of Spain, wrote about Flemish artists who imitated earlier works with the intent to deceive. In this text, *Commentaries on Painting*, he alerted readers that countless pictures of this kind "are signed with the name of Hieronymus Bosch, but are in fact fraudulently inscribed," then smoked in fireplaces, "to lend them credibility and an aged look" (Silver, 2006: 133). This practice reinforced the demand for works in the style of famous or successful artists, especially Bosch. Guevara refers to works created long after the death of their reputed artist. In these situations, where the ties between buyers and sellers were neither abundant nor strong, fraud flourished. (For an example, now attributed to Jan Mandijn, circa 1550, see Figure 40.)

Figure 40 Jan Mandijn, *The Temptation of Saint Anthony*, 1535, oil on panel, Frans Hals Museum, Haarlem. Photo: Wikimedia.

Fakes created a further loss if put on view and detected, as we can see by reading between Guevara's lines. Elsewhere in his treatise, he suggested that King Philip II put his works of art on display, because "paintings that are covered and hidden from view are deprived of their value, which lies in the eyes of others and their judgment by men of understanding and good imagination" (Falomir, 2006: 136). However, if these men of understanding judged the displayed paintings to be fakes or of poor quality, then the reputation of the collector would suffer a hit. The implication: if in doubt, do not display. Phillip II displayed. The King was confident, and rightly so, that he had assembled a superlative collection.

Dealers

Starting in the mid-sixteenth century, when the sale of non-commissioned art increased across Europe, the role of intermediaries grew in importance alongside. Trustworthy dealers assumed risks themselves as a means to reduce the risks of quality and late delivery for buyers. Often, dealers' ties with those who sold them merchandise were neither strong nor extensive. Hence, they bore two significant risks (Rasterhoff and Vermeylen, 2015). First, dealers might overestimate the quality and thus marketability of works, especially when they purchased them in bulk or at auction. Second, they had to hold inventories, which made them vulnerable to purchasers' shifting tastes. Major dealers, such as the Fochondt and Musson firms in the Low Countries, found creative business strategies to reduce risks. In the language of modern finance, they diversified their portfolio of holdings: they obtained paintings of similar subjects at different quality levels or varied in the subject matter and sizes of the offerings. Small-time operators did not have this option. Their holdings were concentrated in a small number of pieces, as our next example makes evident.

In 1618, Hans le Thoor, a jeweler and minor dealer in Amsterdam, consigned six paintings to the painter Pieter Isaacksz, an old acquaintance (Montias, 2002: 144–7). These included two works by Louis Finson, the *Massacre of the Innocents* and the *Four Elements* (Figure 41), which le Thoor had obtained in 1617 from Finson's heirs (Janssen, 2007: 23–4). Isaacksz, who was "painter of the King's chamber" for King Christian IV of Denmark, also served as his agent for foreign purchases. Through the course of a tangle of meetings and communications, le Thoor sent paintings to Isaacksz that the duo felt would appeal to the King. Isaacksz agreed in writing to take responsibility for the paintings and sell them at stipulated prices. He also agreed to pay le Thoor a share of the proceeds and return any unsold paintings within four months. Le Thoor should have been more wary in this first-time relationship with someone only

Figure 41 Louis Finson, *The Four Elements*, 1611, oil on canvas, Museum of
Fine Arts, Houston. Photo: Wikimedia.

tangentially in his network. In short, he got burned. Though le Thoor got some
paintings back, he never received any payment, and he suspected that at least
one of the paintings had been copied, contrary to the agreement. Worse still, he
lost his court case; indeed, he was forced to pay Isaackz's legal fees. Le Thoor
expected to make a killing through sales to the Danish King. That surely helps to
explain his choices despite the tenuous trust.

Conclusion

Two major themes emerge from the scores of hazards discussed in this study.
First, production and reception risks permeated the premodern European art
world. They surely occurred at a far higher and more consequential rate than
accounts of the period would lead us to believe. Careful investigation into risk
shines a light on what could and did go wrong in the production of Renaissance
art. For most purchasers and patrons, the primary concern was for high quality.
For commissioned work, another key issue was timely completion. Efforts to
dial down one of these risks often dialed up the risk on the other. Many people at
the time knew and wrote about these risks, but few if any individuals could
calculate them with any degree of reliability. Uncertainty reigned. Some risks
were taken that should have been foregone; others were foregone that should
have been taken. Consequently, as this Element tallies, bad outcomes were

encountered, and frequently. Some outcomes were not even foreseen as possibilities, meriting our label ignorance. At times, ignorance led to outsize losses, such as the destruction of art. Such events included the collapse of a building wall, a coup tossing the ruling family out of a city, and the Protestant Reformation. Risks not contemplated are risks left untamed.

Our second theme is that the art world flourished in the period 1400–1650 because the Renaissance art business, nestled within the society at large, found many ways to tame such risks. But risk tamed is hardly risk extinguished. Just as Renaissance merchants "developed a sophisticated type of probabilistic reasoning ... to calculate and weigh the potential profits and losses of any particular venture" (Baker, 2021: 90), the key players in the art business weighed informally the risks that affected the benefits and costs of the paintings and sculptures they produced or purchased. They only transacted when they concluded that after considering risks, the benefits – often, a good chance of achieving financial, professional, or social gain – outweighed the expected costs. On the whole, the risky art business of the Renaissance created significant gains for all classes of participants. That is why the production and sale of art thrived. As in other aspects of the economy, risk-taking became another cost of doing business. Painters, patrons, and purchasers all recognized one key tenet: nothing ventured, nothing gained.

The reception risks we have recounted from the premodern era echo today. Not a month passes without news that a painting sold or exhibited as by a famous artist – whether Leonardo da Vinci, Mark Rothko, or Jean-Michel Basquiat – is reputed to be by a student or even a forger. Statues of once-revered leaders have been knocked off their pedestals and sent to warehouses or foundries. Artists still fret that no one will want their products, and patrons still wait for works ordered but not yet delivered. To build on Benjamin Franklin's famous quip on death and taxes: in the art business, the only sure thing is risk.

Bibliography

Agosti, Giovanni. (1989). "Un Giudizio Universale in miniatura." *Annali della Scuola normale superiore di Pisa, Classe di lettere e filosofia* 19 (4): 1291–97.

Aristotle. (1995). *Poetics*. Cambridge, MA: Harvard University Press.

Arnade, Peter. (2008). *Beggars, Iconoclasts, and Civic Patriots: The Political Culture of the Dutch Revolt*. Ithaca: Cornell University Press.

Arroyo Esteban, Santiago. (2013). "'En esto hay muchas opiniones y gustos'. Sobre la fortuna crítica del 'Martirio de San Mauricio' de El Greco." *Reales Sitios* 197: 26–47.

Ashcroft, Jeffrey. (2017). *Albrecht Dürer: Documentary Biography*. New Haven: Yale University Press.

Baker, Nicholas Scott. (2021). *In Fortune's Theater. Financial Risk and the Future in Renaissance Italy*. Cambridge: Cambridge University Press.

Baldwin, Robert. (1986). "Peasant Imagery and Bruegel's 'Fall of Icarus.'" *Konsthistorisk Tidskrift* 55: 101–14.

Bambach, Carmen C. (2019). *Leonardo da Vinci rediscovered*. New Haven: Yale University Press.

Barnes, Bernadine Ann. (1998). *Michelangelo's Last Judgment: The Renaissance Response*. Berkeley: University of California Press.

Bassens, Maarten and Van Grieken, Joris. (2019). *Bruegel: The Complete Graphic Works*. London: Thames & Hudson.

Baxandall, Michael. (1980). *The Limewood Sculptors of Renaissance Germany, 1475–1525*. New Haven: Yale University Press.

Becker, Jochen. (1971). "Hochmut kommt vor dem Fall: Zum Standbild Albas in der Zitadelle von Antwerpen, 1571-1574." *Simiolus* 5 (1/2): 75–115.

Bellhouse, David R. and Franklin, James. (1997). "The Language of Chance." *International Statistical Review* 65: 73–85.

Blier, Suzanne Preston. (2015). *Art and Risk in Ancient Yoruba: Ife History, Power, and Identity, c.1300*. Cambridge: Cambridge University Press.

Bodart, Diane H. (2012). "Il mento 'posticcio' dell'imperatore Carlo V." In Clelia Arcelli, ed. *Estremità e escrescenze del corpo. Extremities and Excrescences of the Body*. Firenze: Sismel Edizioni del Galluzzo: 465–83.

Borsook, Eve. (1970). "Documenti relativi alle cappelle di Lecceto e delle Selve di Filippo Strozzi." *Antichità viva* 9 (3): 3–20.

Bourdieu, Pierre. (1984). *Distinction: A Social Critique of the Judgment of Taste*. Richard Nice, trans. Cambridge, MA: Harvard University Press.

Bourne, Molly. (2007). "Medici Women at the Gonzaga Court, 1584-1627." In Barbara Deimling, Jonathan K. Nelson, Gary M. Radke, eds. *Italian Art, Society, and Politics. A Festschrift for Rab Hatfield*. Firenze: Syracuse University in Florence, 223–43.

Campbell, Lorne. (1985). *The Early Flemish Pictures. The Pictures in the Collection of Her Majesty the Queen*. Cambridge: Cambridge University Press.

Campbell, Stephen J. (2019). *The Endless Periphery: Toward a Geopolitics of Art in Lorenzo Lotto's Italy*. Chicago: University of Chicago Press.

Carlson, Raymond. (2021). "Epistolary Criticism, the Minerva Christ, and Michelangelo's Garzone Problem." In Gamberini, Nelson, and Nova: 126–45.

Carlton, Genevieve. (2015). *Worldly Consumers: The Demand for Maps in Renaissance Italy*. Chicago: University of Chicago Press.

Carroll, Margaret. (1986). "Civic Ideology and Its Subversions: Rembrandt's *Oath of Claudius Civilis*." *Art History* 9 (1): 12–35.

Cavazzini, Patrizia. (2008). *Painting as Business in Early Seventeenth-century Rome*. University Park: Pennsylvania State University Press.

Ceccarelli, Giovanni. (2001). "Risky Business: Theological and Canonical Thought on Insurance from the Thirteenth to the Seventeenth Century." *The Journal of Medieval and Early Modern Studies* 31 (3): 607–58.

Ceccarelli, Giovanni. (2021). *Risky Markets: Marine Insurance in Renaissance Florence*. Leiden: Brill.

Cholcman, Tamar and Maharshak, Dafna. (2014). "Advertising Gone Wrong: Sixtus V in the Image of Moses: The Fontana dell'Acqua Felice as a Failed Communication Channel." *Studies in Visual Arts and Communication* 1 (1). https://journalonarts.org/wp-content/uploads/2015/05/SVACij-Vol1_No1_2014-CHOLCMAN_T-MAHARSHAK_D-Advertising-gone-wrong.pdf.

Chong, Alan. (1987). "The Market for Landscape Painting in Seventeenth-Century Holland." In Peter Sutton, ed. *Masters of 17th-Century Dutch Landscape Painting*. Boston: Museum of Fine Arts, 104–20, 317–32.

Christensen, Carl. (1979). *Art and the Reformation in Germany*. Athens: Ohio University Press.

Ciardi, Roberto Paolo, ed. (1995). *La tribuna del Duomo di Pisa: Capolavori di due secoli*. Milano: Electa.

Cohn, Samuel K. (2021). *Paradoxes of Inequality in Renaissance Italy*. Cambridge: Cambridge University Press.

Coleman, James S. (1990). *Foundations of Social Theory*. Cambridge: Harvard Univesity Press.

Court, Ricardo. (2014). "*De fatigationibus*: What a Merchant's Errant Son Can Teach Us about the Dynamics of Trust." In Grazia Biorci and Ricardo Court, eds. *Il registro di lettere di Giovanni Francesco di Negro (1563–1565): Regole e prospettive di un mondo non clamoroso.* Novi Ligure: Città del silenzio, 49–130.

Crenshaw, Paul. (2001). "Rembrandt's Disputes with his Patrons." *Dutch Crossing* 35 (2): 162–99.

Crenshaw, Paul. (2006). *Rembrandt's Bankruptcy.* Cambridge: Cambridge University Press.

Daniels, Tobias and Esch, Arnold. (2021). "A Donatello for Rome, a Memling for Florence. The maritime transports of the Sermattei of Florence." *Renaissance Studies* 35 (4): 658–74.

Darby, Graham, ed. (2001). *The Origins and Development of the Dutch Revolt.* London: Routledge.

Di Giampaolo, Mario. (1993). *Los frescos italianos de El Escorial.* Madrid: Electa.

Dijk, Sara van. (2015). *"Beauty adorns virtue." Dress in Portraits of Women by Leonardo da Vinci.* PhD dissertation. Leiden: Universiteit Leiden.

du Bourg, Alexis Merle. (2017). *Rubens. The Henri IV Series. (Corpus Rubenianum Ludwig Burchard XIV.2).* Jane MacAvock and Abigail Newman, trans. London: Harvey Miller.

Dunlop, Anne. (2009). *Painted Palaces: The Rise of Secular Art in Early Renaissance Italy.* University Park: Pennsylvania State University Press.

Eckstein, Nicholas A. (2010). "Pittori, amici e vicini: The Formal and Informal Bonds of Community amongst Florentine Artists." In Eckstein and Terpstra: 109–28.

Eckstein, Nicholas A. and Terpstra, Nicholas, eds. (2010). *Sociability and Its Discontents: Civil Society, Social Capital, and Their Alternatives in Late Medieval and Early Modern Europe.* Turnhout: Brepols.

Eire, Carlos. (1986). *War against the Idols: The Reformation of Worship from Erasmus to Calvin.* Cambridge: Cambridge University Press.

Ekserdjian, David. (2006). *Parmigianino.* New Haven: Yale University Press.

Ekserdjian, David. (2021). "Bad Reception and the Renaissance Altarpiece." In Gamberini, Nelson, and Nova: 32–45.

Ewing, Dan. (1990). "Marketing Art in Antwerp, 1460–1560: Our Lady's Pand." *Art Bulletin* 72 (4): 558–84.

Fabri, Ria and Van Hout, Nico, eds. (2009). *From Quinten Metsijs to Peter Paul Rubens: Masterpieces from the Royal Museum Reunited in the Cathedral.* Schoten: BAI.

Falkenburg, Reindert. (1989). "'Alter Einoutus': Over de aard en herkomst van Pieter Aertsens stillevenconceptie." *Nederlands Kunsthistorisch Jaarboek* 40: 41–66.

Falkenburg, Reindert. (1995). "Pieter Aertsen, Rhyparographer." In Jelle Koopmans, Mark Meadow, Kees Meerhoff, and Marijke Spies, eds. *Rhetoric-Rhétoriqueurs-Rederijkers*. Amsterdam: Amsterdam University Press, 197–217.

Falomir, Miguel, ed. (2003). *Tiziano*. Madrid: Museo Nacional del Prado.

Falomir, Miguel. (2006). "Artists' Responses to the Emergence of Markets for Paintings in Spain, c. 1600." In Neil De Marchi and Hans J. Van Miegroet, eds. *Mapping Markets for Paintings in Europe, 1450–1750*. Turnhout: Brepols, 135–63.

Finney, Paul Corby, ed. (1999). *Seeing beyond the Word. Visual Arts and the Calvinist Tradition*. Grand Rapids: Eerdmans.

Fishman, Jane. (1982). *Boerenverdriet: Violence between Peasants and Soldiers in Early Modern Netherlands Art*. Ann Arbor: UMI Research Press.

Franceschini, Chiara. (2021). "Giudizi negativi e stime d'artista nel mondo di Vasari e Michelangelo." In Gamberini, Nelson, and Nova: 46–69.

Franklin, David. (2001). *Painting in Renaissance Florence 1500–1514*. New Haven: Yale University Press.

Franklin, James. (2001). *The Science of Conjecture: Evidence and Probability before Pascal*. Baltimore: Johns Hopkins University Press.

Freedberg, David. (1988). *Iconoclasm and Painting in the Revolt of the Netherlands, 1566–1609*. New York: Garland.

Freedberg, David. (2012). "Art after Iconoclasm. Painting in the Netherlands between 1566 and 1585." In Koenraad Jonckheere and Ruben Suykerbuyk, eds. *Art after Iconoclasm. Painting in the Netherlands between 1566 and 1585*. Turnhout: Brepols, 21–49.

Freedman, Luba. (2015). "Bartolomeo Maranta's 'Discourse' on Titian's 'Annunciation' in Naples: Introduction." *Journal of Art Historiography* 13: 1–48.

Friendly, Michael and Wainer, Howard. (2021). *A History of Data Visualization and Graphic Communication*. Cambridge, MA: Harvard University Press.

Gamberini, Diletta. (2021). "The Fiascos of Mimesis: Ancient Sources for Renaissance Verse Ridiculing Art." In Gamberini, Nelson, and Nova: 70–81.

Gamberini, Diletta, Nelson, Jonathan K., and Nova, Alessandro, eds. (2021). *Bad Reception: Negative Reactions to Italian Renaissance Art*, Special Issue of *Mitteilungen Des Kunsthistorischen Institutes in Florenz* 63 (1).

Gaston, Robert W. (1995). "Sacred Erotica. The Classical Figura in Religious Painting of the Early Cinquecento." *International Journal of the Classical Tradition* 2 (2): 238–64.

Gibson, Walter. (1991). "Bruegel and the Peasants: A Problem of Interpretation." In Walter Gibson, ed. *Pieter Bruegel the Elder: Two Studies*. Lawrence: Spencer Museum, 11–52.

Gilbert, Creighton E. (1992). *Italian Art 1400–1500. Sources and Documents*. Evanston: Northwestern University Press.

Gilbert, Creighton E. (1998). "What Did the Renaissance Patron Buy?" *Renaissance Quarterly* 51 (2): 392–450.

Goldberg, Edward L. (1992). "Spanish Taste, Medici Politics and a Lost Chapter in the History of Cigoli's 'Ecce Homo.'" *The Burlington Magazine* 134: 102–10.

Goldberg, Gisela, Heimberg, Bruno, and Schawe, Martin, eds. (1998). *Albrecht Dürer: Die Gemälde der Alte Pinakothek*. Heidelberg: Braus.

Goldgar, Anne. (2007). *Tulipmania. Money, Honor, and Knowledge in the Dutch Golden Age*. Chicago: University of Chicago Press.

Gombrich, Ernst H. (1976). "The Leaven of Criticism in Renaissance Art: Texts and Episodes." In *The Heritage of Apelles. Studies in the Art of the Renaissance*. Ithaca: Cornell University Press, 111–31.

González García, Juan Luis. (2018). "'It did not please His Majesty': Philip II and the Habsburg Taste for Italian Renaissance Art." Paper presented at the Kunsthistorisches Institute, Florence.

Granovetter, Mark S. (1973). "The Strength of Weak Ties." *American Journal of Sociology* 78: 1360–80.

Greengrass, Mark. (2014). *Christendom Destroyed. Europe 1517–1648*. New York: Viking.

Greif, Avner. (1989). "Reputation and Coalitions in Medieval Trade: Evidence on the Maghribi Traders." *Journal of Economic History* 49: 857–82.

Held, Julius. (1969). *Rembrandt's Aristotle, and Other Rembrandt Studies*. Princeton: Princeton University Press.

Held, Julius. (1980). *The Oil Sketches of Peter Paul Rubens*. Princeton: Princeton University Press.

Helmstutler Di Dio, Kelley. (2015). "Shipping Sculptures, Shaping Diplomacy: Gifts of Sculpture for Spain." In Kelley Helmstutler Di Dio, ed. *Making and Moving Sculpture in Early Modern Italy*. Farnham and Burlington: Ashgate, 167–90.

Hendler, Sefy. (2021). "'Broken into Pieces and Its Head Thrown into the Square': The Numerous Failures of Michelangelo's Bronze Statue of Pope Julius II." In Gamberini, Nelson, and Nova 115–26.

Herlihy, David and Christiane Klapisch-Zuber. (1985). *Tuscans and Their Families: A Study of the Florentine Catasto of 1427*. New Haven: Yale University Press.

Heuer, Christopher. (2012). "Entropic Segers." *Art History* 35: 935–57.

Hofmann, Werner, ed. (1983). *Luther und die Folgen für die Kunst*. München: Prestel-Verlag.

Holmes, Megan. (2003). "Neri di Bicci and the Commodification of Artistic Values." In Marcello Fantoni, Louisa Chevalier Matthew, and Sara Matthews Grieco, eds. *The Art Market in Italy: 15th-17th Centuries*. Ferrara: Pannini, 213–23.

Honig, Elizabeth. (1998). *Painting and the Market in Early Modern Antwerp*. New Haven: Yale University Press.

Howard, Peter and Hewlett, Cecilia, eds. (2016). *Studies on Florence and the Italian Renaissance in Honour of F.W. Kent*. Turnhout: Brepols.

Hub, Berthold. (2011). "Founding and Ideal City in Filarete's *Libro Architettonico*." In Minou Schraven and Maarten Delbeke, eds. *Foundation, Dedication and Consecration in Early Modern Europe*. Leiden: Brill, 17–58.

Hunt, John M. (2016). *The Vacant See in Early Modern Rome. A Social History of the Papal Interregnum*. Boston and Leiden: Brill.

Isabella d'Este. (2017). *Selected Letters*. Deanna Shemek, ed. and trans. Toronto: Iter Press.

Israel, Jonathan. (1997). "Adjusting to Hard Times: Dutch Art during its Period of Crisis and Restructuring (c.1621–c.1645)." *Art History* 20: 449–76.

Janssen, Paul Huys. (2007). "'The Four Elements' by Louis Finson: A Rediscovered Masterpiece." In Paul Smeets, ed. *Louis Finson: The Four Elements*. Milano: Rob Smeets, 13–26.

Jonckheere, Koenraad. (2012). *Antwerp Art after Iconoclasm. Experiments in Decorum 1566–1585*. Brussels: Mercatorfonds.

Jonckheere, Koenraad. (2014). "An Allegory of Artistic Choice in Times of Trouble: Pieter Bruegel's *Tower of Babel*." *Nederlands Kunsthistorisch Jaarboek* 64: 151–77.

Jost, Ingrid. (1964). "Bemerkungen zur Heinrichsgalerie des P.P. Rubens." *Nederlands Kunsthistorisch Jaarboek* 15: 175–219.

Kahneman, Daniel and Tversky, Amos. (1974). "Judgment under Uncertainty: Heuristics and Biases." *Science* 185 (4157): 1124–31.

Kahneman, Daniel and Tversky, Amos. (1979). "Prospect Theory: An Analysis of Decision under Risk." *Econometrica* 47 (2): 263–91.

Kahsnitz, Rainer, ed. (1983). *Veit Stoss in Nürnberg: Werke des Meisters und seiner Schule in Nürnberg und Umgebung*. München: Deutscher Kunstverlag, 1983.

Kahsnitz, Rainer, ed. (2006). *Carved Splendor: Late Gothic Altarpieces in Southern Germany, Austria and South Tirol*. Russel Stockman, trans. Los Angeles: J. Paul Getty Museum.

Kaplan, Paul H. D. (1997). "Veronese and the Inquisition: The Geopolitical Context." In Elizabeth C. Childs, ed. *Suspended License: Censorship and the Visual Arts*. Seattle: University of Washington Press, 85–124.

Kavaler, Ethan. (1986). "Bruegel's *Fall of Icarus* and the Noble Peasant." *Jaarboek Koninklijk Museum voor Schone Kunsten Antwerpen*: 83–98.

Kavaler, Ethan. (1999). *Pieter Bruegel. Parables of Order and Enterprise*. Cambridge: Cambridge University Press.

Kent, Dale. (2000). *Cosimo de' Medici and the Florentine Renaissance: The Patron's Oeuvre*. New Haven: Yale University Press.

Kirby, Jo. (2000). "The Price of Quality: Factors Influencing the Cost of Pigments during the Renaissance." In Gabriele Neher and Rupert Shepherd, eds. *Revaluing Renaissance Art*. Aldershot: Ashgate, 19–42.

Klapisch-Zuber, Christiane. (1985). "Kin, Friends, and Neighbors: The Urban Territory of a Merchant Family in 1400." In Christiane Klapisch-Zuber, ed. *Women, Family and Ritual in Renaissance Italy*. Lydia G. Cochrane, trans. Chicago: Chicago University Press, 68–93.

Kloek, Wouter Th. and Halsema-Kubes, Willy, eds. (1986). *Kunst voor de Beeldenstorm. Noordnederlandse kunst 1525–1580*. 's-Gravenhage: Staatsuitgeverij.

Knight, Frank H. (1921). *Risk, Uncertainty and Profit*. Boston: Houghton Mifflin.

Kunzle, David. (2002). *From Criminal to Courtier: The Soldier in Netherlandish Art, 1550–1672*. Leiden: Brill.

Kurz, Otto. (1948). *Fakes: A Handbook for Collectors and Students*. New Haven: Yale University Press.

Leeflang, Huigen and Luijten, Ger, eds. (2004). *Hendrick Goltzius (1558–1617): Drawings, Prints and Paintings*. Zwolle: Waanders.

Leeflang, Huigen and Roelofs, Pieter, eds. (2016). *Hercules Segers: Painter, Etcher*. Amsterdam: Rijksmuseum.

Lugli, Emanuele. (2023). *Measuring in the Renaissance: An Introduction*. Cambridge: Cambridge University Press.

Luhmann, Niklas. (1988). "Familiarity, Confidence, Trust: Problems and Alternatives." In Diego Gambetta, ed. *Trust: Making and Breaking Cooperative Relations*. New York: Blackwell, 94–108.

Luhmann, Niklas. (2002). *Risk: A Sociological Theory*. New York: Routledge.

Maffei, Sonia. (2017). "Giovanni Andrea Gilio e il *Dialogo de gli errori et abusi de' pittori* tra licenza e sprezzatura." *Annali di critica d'arte* 1: 145–59.

Mancinelli, Fabrizio. (1997). "The Painting of the *Last Judgment*: History, Technique, and Restoration." In *Michelangelo–the Last Judgment: A Glorious Restoration*. New York: Harry N. Abrams, 187–204.

Marnef, Guido. (1996). *Antwerp in the Age of Reformation: Underground Protestantism in a Commercial Metropolis, 1550–1577*. Baltimore: Johns Hopkins University Press.

McCall, Timothy. (2018). "Material Fictions of Luxury in Sforza Milan." In Catherine Kovesi, ed. *Luxury and the Ethics of Greed in Early Modern Italy*. Turnhout: Brepols, 239–76.

Mclean, Alick M. (2015). "Don't Screw with the Law: Visual and Spatial Defences against Judicial and Political Corruption in Communal Italy." In Peter Goodrich and Valérie Hayaery, eds. *Genealogies of Legal Vision*. London: Routledge, 179–200.

Melli, Lorenza. (1999). "A New Investigation on the Preparatory Drawing for the Equestrian Monument to John Hawkwood by Paolo Uccello: Its Genesis and Relationship with the Fresco." In Hélène Verougstraete and Rogier Van Schoute, eds. *La peinture dans les Pays-Bas au 16e siècle*. Leuven: Peters, 261–72.

Millen, Ronald Forsyth and Wolf, Robert Eric. (1989). *Heroic Deeds and Mystic Figures. A New Reading of Rubens's Life of Maria de' Medici*. Princeton: Princeton University Press.

Mochizuki, Mia. (2008). *The Netherlandish Image after Iconoclasm, 1566–1672: Material Religion in the Dutch Golden Age*. Aldershot and Burlington: Ashgate.

Montias, John Michael. (1987). "Cost and Value in Seventeenth-Century Dutch Art." *Art History* 10: 455–66.

Montias, John Michael. (1989). *Vermeer and his Milieu: A Web of Social History*. Princeton: Princeton University Press.

Montias, John Michael. (1990). "The Influence of Economic Factors on Style." *De zeventiende eeuw* 6: 49–57.

Montias, John Michael. (2002). *Art at Auction in 17th Century Amsterdam*. Amsterdam: Amsterdam University Press.

Morselli, Raffaella. (2010). "Bologna." In Richard E. Spear and Philip Sohm, eds. *Painting for Profit: The Economic Lives of Seventeenth-Century Italian Painters*. New Haven: Yale University Press, 145–71.

Moxey, Keith. (1977). *Pieter Aertsen, Joachim Beuckelaer, and the Rise of Secular Painting in the Context of the Reformation*. New York: Garland.

Mozzati, Tommaso. (2008). *Giovanfrancesco Rustici. Le Compagnie del Paiuolo e della Cazzuola*. Firenze: Leo. S. Olschki.

Müller, Jürgen and Schauerte, Thomas, eds. (2011). *Die gottlosen Maler von Nürnberg: Konvention und Subversion in der Druckgrafik der Beham-Brüder*. Emsdetten: Edition Imorde.

Nelson, Jonathan K. (2002). "The Florentine Venus and Cupid: A Heroic Female Nude and the Power of Love." In Franca Falletti and Jonathan K. Nelson, eds.

Venus and Cupid. Michelangelo and the New Ideal of Beauty/ Venere e Amore. Michelangelo e la nuova bellezza ideale. Firenze: Giunti, 26–63.

Nelson, Jonathan K. (2004). "La disgrazia di Pietro: l'importanza della pala della Santissima Annunziata nella Vita del Perugino del Vasari." In Laura Teza, ed. *Pietro Vannucci il Perugino.* Perugia: Volumnia Editrice, 65–73.

Nelson, Jonathan K. (2022). *Filippino Lippi: An Abundance of Invention.* London: Reaktion Books.

Nelson, Jonathan K. and Zeckhauser, Richard J. (2008). *The Patron's Payoff: Conspicuous Commissions in Italian Renaissance Art.* Princeton: Princeton University Press.

Nelson, Jonathan K. and Zeckhauser, Richard J. (2018). "Raphael, Superstar, and His Extraordinary Prices." *Source: Notes in the History of Art* 38 (1): 15–23.

Nelson, Jonathan K. and Zeckhauser, Richard J. (2021). "Italian Renaissance Portraits that Disappoint: Isabelle d'Este, Francesco del Giocondo and Other Disgruntled Patrons." In Gamberini, Nelson, and Nova: 15–31.

Newman, Abigail and Nijkamp, Lieneke, eds. (2021). *Many Antwerp Hands: Collaborations in Netherlandish Art.* Turnhout: Brepols.

North, Michael. (1997). *Art and Commerce in the Dutch Golden Age.* Catherine Hill, trans. New Haven: Yale University Press.

Nova, Alessandro. (2021). "Bad Reception in Early Modern Italy: An Introduction." In Gamberini, Nelson, and Nova: 7–14.

Nygren, Christopher J. (2017). "Titian's *Ecce Homo* on Slate: Stone, Oil, and the Transubstantiation of Painting." *The Art Bulletin* 99 (1): 36–66.

Nygren, Christopher J. (2021). "Sedimentary Aesthetics." In Lauren Jacobi and Daniel Zolli, eds. *Contamination and Purity in Early Modern Art and Architecture.* Amsterdam: Amsterdam University Press, 129–56.

O'Malley, Michelle. (2005). *The Business of Art: Contracts and the Commissioning Process in Renaissance Italy.* New Haven: Yale University Press.

Orenstein, Nadine, ed. (2001). *Pieter Bruegel the Elder Drawings and Prints.* New Haven: Yale University Press.

Origo, Iris. (1957). *The Merchant of Prato.* New York: Alfred A. Knopf.

Ostrow, Steven F. (2006). "The Discourse of Failure in Seventeenth-Century Rome: Prospero Bresciano's *Moses.*" *The Art Bulletin* 88 (2): 267–91.

Padgett, John F. (2010). "Open Elite? Social Mobility, Marriage, and Family in Florence, 1282-1494." *Renaissance Quarterly* 63 (2): 357–411.

Pelham, Georgina. (2000). "Reconstructing the Programme of the Tomb of Guido Tarlati, Bishop and Lord of Arezzo." In Joanna Cannon and Beth Williamson, eds. *Art, Politics and Civic Religion in Central Italy, 1261–1352: Essays by*

Postgraduate Students at the Courtauld Institute of Art. Aldershot: Ashgate, 71–115.

Piazza, Filippo. (2018). "Tiziano e le tele della Loggia di Brescia: cronaca di una disavventura." In Francesco Frangi, ed. *Tiziano e la pittura del Cinquecento tra Venezia e Brescia.* Silvana: Cinisello Balsamo, 178–99.

Price, David. (2003). *Dürer's Renaissance.* Ann Arbor: University of Michigan Press.

Pym, Anthony. (2015). "Translating as Risk Management." *Journal of Pragmatics* 85: 67–80.

Ramsey, Frank P. (1931). "Truth and Probability." In Frank Ramsey and Richard B. Braithwaite, eds. *The Foundations of Mathematics and Other Logical Essays.* London: Kegan, Paul, Trench, Trubner, 156–98.

Rasterhoff, Claartje. (2016). "Economic Aspects of Dutch Art." In Wayne Franits, ed. *The Ashgate Research Companion to Dutch Art of the Seventeenth Century.* London: Routledge, 355–71.

Rasterhoff, Claartje and Vermeylen, Filip. (2015). "Mediators of Trade and Taste: Dealing with Demand and Quality Uncertainty in the International Art Markets of the Seventeenth Century." *De Zeventiende Eeuw* 31 (1): 138–58.

Raupp, Hans-Joachim. (1986). *Bauernsatiren.* Niederzier: Lukassen.

Reichlin, Susanne. (2019). "Risiko und âventiure. Die Faszination für das ungesicherte Wagnis im historischen Wandel." In Scheller: 13–32.

Reiss, Sheryl E. (2013). "A Taxonomy of Art Patronage in Renaissance Italy." In Babette Bohn and James M. Saslow, eds. *A Companion to Renaissance and Baroque Art.* Chichester: Wiley-Blackwell, 23–43.

Renger, Konrad and Denk, Claudia. (2002). *Flämische Malerei des Barock in der Alten Pinakothek.* München: Pinakothek-DuMont.

Rizzi, Andrea, Lang, Birgit, and Pym, Anthony. (2019). *What is Translation History? A Trust-Based Approach.* Cham: Palgrave Macmillan.

Ronen, Avraham. (1970). "Portigiani's Bronze 'Ornamento' in the Church of the Holy Sepulchre, Jerusalem." *Mitteilungen des Kunsthistorischen Institutes in Florenz* 14 (4): 415–42.

Roper, Lyndal. (2017). *Martin Luther. Renegade and Prophet.* New York: Random House.

Roy, Devjani and Zeckhauser, Richard. (2015). "Grappling with Ignorance: Frameworks from Decision Theory, Lessons from Literature." *Journal of Benefit-Cost Analysis* 6 (1): 33–65.

Rubin, Patricia Lee. (1995). *Giorgio Vasari. Art and History.* New Haven: Yale University Press.

Russo, Alessandra. (2011). "Postface: Uncatchable Colors." In Gerhard Wolf and Joseph Connors, eds. *Colors Between Two Worlds: The Florentine codex of Bernardino de Sahagun*. Firenze: Villa I Tatti, The Harvard University Center for Italian Renaissance Studies, 389–412.

Scheller, Benjamin, ed. (2019a). *Kulturen des Risikos im Mittelalter und in der Frühen Neuzeit*. Berlin: De Gruyter.

Scheller, Benjamin. (2019b). "Einführende Bemerkungen." In Scheller: 1–12.

Schreurs, Anna. (2000). *Antikenbild und Kunstanschauungen des neapolitanischen Malers, Architekten und Antiquars Pirro Ligorio (1513–1583)*. Köln: Walther König.

Schwartz, Daniel. (2019). *The Political Morality of the Late Scholastics Civic Life, War and Conscience*. Cambridge: Cambridge University Press.

Signorini, Rodolfo. (1974). "Federico III e Cristiano I nella Camera degli Sposi del Mantegna." *Mitteilungen des Kunsthistorischen Institutes in Florenz* 18: 227–50.

Silver, Larry. (1996). "Pieter Bruegel in the Capital of Capitalism." *Nederlands Kunsthistorisch Jaarboek* 47: 125–53.

Silver, Larry. (2006). *Peasant Scenes and Landscapes: The Rise of Pictorial Genres in the Antwerp Art Market*. Philadelphia: University of Pennsylvania Press.

Silver, Larry. (2008). "Visual Art as Self-Advertising (Europe and America)." In Jonathan K. Nelson and Richard J. Zeckhauser, eds. *The Patron's Payoff: Conspicuous Commissions in Italian Renaissance Art*. Princeton: Princeton University Press, 186–92.

Silver, Larry. (2013). "Cultural Selection and the Shape of Time." In Barbara Larson and Sabine Flach, eds. *Darwin and Theories of Aesthetics and Cultural History*. Farnham: Ashgate, 69–82.

Silver, Larry. (2014). "Bruegel's Biblical Kings." In Walter Melion, James Clifton, and Michel Weemans, eds. *Imago exegetica. Visual Images as Exegetical Instruments, 1400–1700*. Leiden: Brill, 791–831.

Silver, Larry. (2015). "Morbid Fascination: Death by Bruegel." In Walter Melion, Bret Rothstein, and Michel Weemans, eds. *The Anthropomorphic Lens: Anthropomorphism and Analogy in Early Modern Thought and Visual Arts*. Leiden: Brill, 421–54.

Sluijter, Eric Jan. (1996). "Jan van Goyen als marktleider, virtuoos en vernieuwer." In Christiaan Vogelaar, ed. *Jan van Goyen*. Leiden: Lakenhal, 38–59.

Sluijter, Eric Jan. (2009). "On Brabant Rubbish, Economic Competition, Artistic Rivalry, and the Growth of the Market for Paintings in the First Decades of the Seventeenth Century." *Journal of the Historians of Netherlandish Art* 1 (2). DOI: 10.5092/jhna.2009.1.2.4.

Smith, Jeffrey Chipps. (1985). "The Transformation in Patrician Tastes in Renaissance Nuremberg," In Jeffery Chipps Smith, ed. *New Perspectives on the Art of Renaissance Nuremberg*. Austin: Huntington Gallery, 83–100.

Smyth, Carolyn. (1997). *Correggio's Frescoes in Parma Cathedral*. Princeton: Princeton University Press.

Spagnolo, Maddalena. (2021). "Effimere saette: sfide e limiti di una Kunstliteratur satiricoburlesca." In Gamberini, Nelson, and Nova: 83–98.

Springer, Carolyn. (2010). *Armour and Masculinity in the Italian Renaissance*. Toronto: University of Toronto Press.

Stoesser, Alison. (2018). *Van Dyck's Hosts in Genoa: Lucas and Cornelis De Wael's Lives, Business Activities and Works*. Turnhout: Brepols.

Strauss, Gerald. (1976). *Nuremberg in the Sixteenth Century*. Bloomington: Indiana University Press.

Tobey, Tracy E. (2013). "'Damnatio memoriae': The Rebirth of Condemnation of Memory in Renaissance Florence." *Renaissance and Reformation/ Renaissance et Réforme* 36 (3): 5–32

Unverfehrt, Gerd. (1980). *Hieronymus Bosch: Die Rezeption seiner Werk im frühen 16. Jahrhundert*. Berlin: Mann.

Van de Waal, Henri. (1974). "The Iconographical Background to Rembrandt's *Civilis*." In Rudolf Herman Fuchs, ed. *Steps Toward Rembrandt: Collected Articles 1937–1972*. Patricia Wardle and Alan Griffiths, trans. Amsterdam: North-Holland, 44–72.

Van der Coelen, Peter and Lammertse, Friso. (2015). *De ontdekking van het dagelijks leven: van Bosch tot Bruegel*. Rotterdam: Museum Boijmans Van Beuningen.

Van Grieken, Joris, Luijten, Ger, and Van der Stock, Jan, eds. (2013). *Hieronymus Cock: The Renaissance in Print*. Brussels: Mercatorfonds.

Van Hoogstraten, Samuel. (2021). *Introduction to the Academy of Painting; or The Visible World* [1678]. Celeste Brusati, ed. Jaap Jacobs, trans. Los Angeles: Getty Research Institute.

Van Kessel, Elsje. (2017). *The Lives of Paintings: Presence, Agency and Likeness in Venetian Art of the Sixteenth Century*. Boston: De Gruyter.

Van Mander, Karel. (1994). *The Lives of the Illustrious Netherlandish and German Painters* [1603–4], Hessel Miedema, ed. and trans. Doornspijk: Davaco.

Vasari, Giorgi. (1912–15). *Lives of the Most Eminent Painters, Sculptors and Architects* [1568]. Gaston de C. de Vere, trans. London: Macmillan.

Vergara, Alejandro, ed. (2007). *Patinir: Essays and Critical Catalogue*. Madrid: Museo Nacional del Prado.

Vermeylen, Filip. (2003). *Painting for the Market: Commercialization of Art in Antwerp's Golden Age*. Turnhout: Brepols.

Vermeylen, Filip and Van der Stichelenm, Katlijne. (2006). "The Antwerp Guild of Saint Luke and the Marketing of Paintings, 1400-1700." In Neil

De Marchi and Hans J. Van Miegroet, eds. *Mapping Markets for Paintings in Europe, 1450–1750*. Turnhout: Brepols, 189–208.

Von Klarwill, Victor. (1928). *Queen Elizabeth and Some Foreigners*. T. H. Nash, trans. London: John Lane.

Williams, Robert. (1993). "The Facade of the Palazzo dei 'Visacci.'" *I Tatti Studies* 5: 209–44.

Woodall, Joanna. (2016). *Anthonis Mor. Art and Authority*. Leiden: Brill.

Woods-Marsden, Joanna. (1987). "'Ritratto al Natural': Questions of Realism and Idealism in Early Renaissance Portraits." *Art Journal* 46 (3): 209–16.

Zarucchi, Jeanne Morgan. (2013). "Perrault's Memoirs and Bernini: A Reconsideration." *Renaissance Studies* 27 (3): 356–70.

Zeckhauser, Richard. (2006). "Investing in the Unknown and Unknowable." *Capitalism and Society* 1 (2): 1–39.

Acknowledgments

Our work on the risks of Renaissance art started more than two decades ago, growing out of the research for our previous book, *The Patron's Payoff*. Though we cannot possibly cite the large number of colleagues who have provided advice and examples over many years, it is important to acknowledge at least those who read materials from the present study and provided useful suggestions. They are Nic Baker, Jim Franklin, Diletta Gamberini, John Henderson, Sefy Hendler, Dave Johnson, Emanuele Lugli, and Daniel Wang. We are also most grateful for the conscientious and insightful research assistance by Harleen Bagga, Justin Chan, and Sharifa Lookman.

Cambridge Elements ☰

The Renaissance

John Henderson

Birkbeck, University of London, and Wolfson College, University of Cambridge

John Henderson is Emeritus Professor of Italian Renaissance History at Birkbeck, University of London, and Emeritus Fellow of Wolfson College, University of Cambridge. His recent publications include *Florence Under Siege: Surviving Plague in an Early Modern City* (2019), and *Plague and the City*, edited with Lukas Engelmann and Christos Lynteris (2019), and *Representing Infirmity: Diseased Bodies in Renaissance Italy*, edited with Fredrika Jacobs and Jonathan K. Nelson (2021). He is also the author of *Piety and Charity in Late Medieval Florence* (1994); *The Great Pox: The French Disease in Renaissance Europe*, with Jon Arrizabalaga and Roger French (1997); and *The Renaissance Hospital: Healing the Body and Healing the Soul* (2006). Forthcoming publications include a Cambridge Element, *Representing and Experiencing the Great Pox in Renaissance Italy* (2023).

Jonathan K. Nelson

Syracuse University Florence

Jonathan K. Nelson teaches Italian Renaissance Art at Syracuse University Florence and is research associate at the Harvard Kennedy School. His books include *Filippino Lippi* (2004, with Patrizia Zambrano); *Leonardo e la reinvenzione della figura femminile* (2007); *The Patron's Payoff: Conspicuous Commissions in Italian Renaissance Art* (2008, with Richard J. Zeckhauser); *Filippino Lippi* (2022); and he co-edited *Representing Infirmity: Diseased Bodies in Renaissance Italy* (2021). He co-curated museum exhibitions dedicated to Michelangelo (2002), Botticelli and Filippino (2004), Robert Mapplethorpe (2009), and Marcello Guasti (2019), and two online exhibitions about Bernard Berenson (2012, 2015).

Assistant Editor

Editorial Board

About the Series

Timely, concise, and authoritative, Elements in the Renaissance showcases cutting-edge scholarship by both new and established academics. Designed to introduce students, researchers, and general readers to key questions in current research, the volumes take multi-disciplinary and transnational approaches to explore the conceptual, material, and cultural frameworks that structured Renaissance experience.

Cambridge Elements ☰

The Renaissance

Elements in the Series

Milton Keynes UK
Ingram Content Group UK Ltd.
UKHW010850140324
439422UK00010B/74